OUR TRIP AROUND THE WORLD

OUR TRIP AROUND THE WORLD

BY RENATE BELCZYK

RMB

For information on purchasing bulk quantities of this book, or to obtain media excerpts or invite the author to speak at an event, please visit rmbooks.com and select the "Contact" tab.

RMB | Rocky Mountain Books Ltd.
rmbooks.com
@rmbooks
facebook.com/rmbooks

Cataloguing data available from Library and Archives Canada
ISBN 9781771603775 (paperback)
ISBN 9781771603782 (electronic)

Printed and bound in Canada

We would like to also take this opportunity to acknowledge the traditional territories upon which we live and work. In Calgary, Alberta, we acknowledge the Niitsítapi (Blackfoot) and the people of the Treaty 7 region in Southern Alberta, which includes the Siksika, the Piikuni, the Kainai, the Tsuut'ina and the Stoney Nakoda First Nations, including Chiniki, Bearpaw, and Wesley First Nations. The City of Calgary is also home to Métis Nation of Alberta, Region III. In Victoria, British Columbia, we acknowledge the traditional territories of the Lkwungen (Esquimalt, and Songhees), Malahat, Pacheedaht, Scia'new, T'Sou-ke and W̱SÁNEĆ (Pauquachin, Tsartlip, Tsawout, Tseycum) peoples.

We acknowledge the financial support of the Government of Canada through the Canada Book Fund and the Canada Council for the Arts, and of the province of British Columbia through the British Columbia Arts Council and the Book Publishing Tax Credit.

To Sigrid's and my grandchildren,
Rebecca, Benjamin, Zachary, Sebastian, Zoe,
Gabriel, Gabriella, Skylar, Lukas and Teya.
May you see as much and more than we did
of this wonderful world.

CONTENTS

FOREWORD
BY CHIC SCOTT

"Security is mostly a superstition. It does not exist in nature,
nor do the children of humankind as a whole experience it.
Avoiding danger is no safer in the long run than outright exposure.
Life is either a daring adventure, or it is nothing at all."

—HELEN KELLER

Renate Belczyk is a remarkable woman. Positive and good natured, she is still downhill skiing at 88 years of age. She has travelled the world, climbed mountains, raised a family and now she has written her book.

Renate's trip around the world with her childhood friend Sigrid Hirte, in the years 1955 to 1958, was simply an amazing adventure. At that time very few young women went off on their own into foreign lands. That they made this journey with no serious incidents speaks volumes for their ability to adapt, befriend the locals and appreciate their cultures. Reading Renate's book I am reminded of the words of Freya Stark, a great adventurer of the 1930s:

"If I were asked to enumerate the pleasures of travel, this would be one of the greatest among them — that so often and so unexpectedly you meet the best in human nature, and seeing it so by surprise and often with a most improbable background, you come, with a sense of pleasant thankfulness, to realize how widely scattered in the world are goodness and courtesy and the love of immaterial things, fair blossoms found in every climate, on every soil."

Their adventure begins in Mexico, where they befriended local mountain climbers and reached the top of several of the largest volcanoes. In this country they worked to pay their way, learned the language and made many friends. One of these young Mexican climbers even offered Renate marriage (which was refused). In later years this fellow would name his children Renate and Sigrid in their honour.

Here in Canada their climb of Mount Victoria to honour their Mexican friends who had perished on the mountain two years earlier was an outstanding feat. And then their adventure in the Little Yoho Valley with Hans Gmoser in 1957 where they played a role in the development of mountain skiing in Canada. That ski camp at the Stanley Mitchell Hut would lead eventually to the creation of Canadian Mountain Holidays and the world famous heli ski empire. Although it is not explained in the book, Renate told me that she and Sigrid got off the train in Field, BC, and found their way to the Little Yoho by themselves. These young women seemed not to need guides.

A chance meeting in the Vancouver Harbour with Japanese sailors took them to Japan, where they rode bicycles around the main Islands of the country. They soon become celebrities in the local media and were eventually offered motor scooters to aid them on their way.

The highlight of the book is perhaps their drive across India on their scooters, visiting remote Nepal en route. Camping wild and living simply, they took what looks today like big risks. But at that time young female travellers, particularly European, would have been regarded largely with curiosity and amusement and would have had more security.

Renate and Sigrid were lucky to have the opportunity to experience the world before globalization largely homogenized our diverse cultures. And they were lucky to do so without misadventure, for it certainly was a dangerous undertaking at times. They wandered the Valley of the Kings in Egypt, largely on their own, and drove their motor scooters through Turkey, across Macedonia and through the Balkans to Germany. Everywhere they went they were welcomed with kindness and helped by the locals.

Renate and Sigrid are still the best of friends today and visit often, sometimes in person and sometimes by telephone. They have both lived rich and interesting lives and acquired the wisdom that comes with age.

Renate's story was written for her grandchildren but it is also a gift to us. Her example to us – be positive, open your heart, take a chance and explore the world – is still valid. I hope this book inspires and gives courage to young people of today.

—Chic Scott
Banff, 2020.

PREFACE

Ever since the war ended in 1945, and the rebuilding of Germany began, my friend Sigrid and I had dreamt about foreign cities such as Rome and Istanbul, Paris and Moscow, or even such faraway places as Calcutta, Kathmandu or Hong Kong. Very little travelling was done by anyone in those difficult years. Yet we were obsessed with seeing the world.

In 1948, after investing months getting the necessary permits, Sigrid and I spent our summer holiday in Italy, bicycling on our ancient, prewar, one-gear bicycles all the way from Frankfurt to Naples and back. Very few cars were on the road then and we had a wonderful time. Our next trip was to England. In 1951 we hired out as nannies and stayed for a year in London to improve on our school English and to see as much as possible of England, Scotland and Ireland.

As we were still planning to travel the world, we decided it might be also useful to improve our French language skills. In the spring of 1953, we bought three-gear bicycles – the latest in bike technology – and set off for France. For eight months we bicycled all over the country and enjoyed the land and the people. Whenever we ran out of money, we worked: four weeks as chambermaids in a Paris hotel, another four weeks in Southern France during the wine harvest. As grape pickers we not only earned our wages but also a bottle of wine every day. By the time the grapes were picked, and the wine drunk, it was late fall, and we spent the rest of the year bicycling through Spain and Portugal. We had planned to go on to Africa, but Sigrid's mother became ill and she wanted Sigrid to come home. Reluctantly, we boarded a train and went back to Frankfurt.

Once home, we both got jobs, worked hard and saved as much as we could. Our next plan was to go to Mexico. One reason for this decision was that Sigrid had relatives there. We'd also formed a romantic notion of this country from reading travel and adventure books. Finally, the idea of travelling to another continent appealed to us. In the summer of 1955, we left Germany for Mexico and returned three adventurous years later.

Even after these travels together, Sigrid and I seemed fated to be like-minded. Each of us got married in September 1960, Sigrid in Freiburg, Germany, and I in Field, BC. To this day, Sigrid and I continue to see each other almost once every year.

I translated from German the diary of Sigrid's and my journey around the world from 1955 to 1958. On behalf of Sigrid and myself, I dedicate this book to you, our grandchildren. I hope you enjoy it. I know we had a slight advantage over you because mass tourism had not been invented yet, but there is still a lot to see and discover. I wish you an open mind, joy and happiness.

Much love to you all,
Your grandmother, Renate
—Summer 2005

CHAPTER 1

EARLY YEARS

I was born in Dresden, Germany, in 1932. When I was 3 years old, my parents, together with my older sister Ingrid and me, moved to Berlin. We settled into a small apartment building in the outskirts of the city. A forest surrounded the place and the river Spree, with its nice sandy beach, was only a short distance away. In the apartment below us lived Sigrid. We became friends right away and stayed that way. Sigrid and I climbed trees, learned to swim, played together and eventually entered school. Just then the war started, and I loved it when there was an alarm during the night and we didn't have to go to school until 10 a.m. instead of 8 a.m. I also loved to watch the bombers during the night when the sky was ablaze with light.

Because of the constant bombing in Berlin, all elementary schools were closed in 1943. My mother, Ingrid and I were sent to a small village, Milmersdorf, 60 kilometres east of the city. Sigrid and her parents moved south to her grandparents, but we stayed in touch. My father continued working in Berlin but visited every weekend. For Christmas all our friends in the apartment house decided to come back to Berlin to celebrate the holidays together. It was a big mistake. On Christmas Eve bombers hit our area, and when we finally got out of the cellar we found every window blown out and some of the walls broken down. Mother had saved for a long time for special ingredients to bake a wonderful Christmas cake. It was completely covered with splinters of glass. "Can't we take the glass out?" I begged my mother, but she took the cake and threw it in the garbage. Ingrid and I were then sent back to Milmersdorf while my parents stayed back for a few days to clean up the mess and cover the windows with cardboard.

In order to attend school, we had to drive ten kilometres by bus every day, but that also soon ended. The Russian army was approaching and we heard the shooting day and night. Through the firm my father worked for, he organized a bus and together with some other families we were transported west. It was a long and difficult trip. Because of the bombing by low-flying planes, we had to travel mostly by night and with barely enough light to see the road. We finally ended up in Southern Germany in a place called Nusplingen. The three of us had one room and shared the kitchen as well as the outhouse.

Then the war ended and Americans occupied our village. The first time I dared to go outside, two American soldiers walked ahead of me. Suddenly, one turned around and put his hand in his pocket. I was 100 percent sure he was going to shoot me, but he handed me a chocolate bar instead. I have loved Americans ever since.

In 1948, during the next summer holidays, Ingrid and I biked on our old one-speed bikes to Bavaria to meet Sigrid there. It was so good to be together again. We biked around to see castles like Neuschwanstein, cathedrals, museums and other beautiful places. We also climbed the highest mountain in Germany, the Zugspitze. We were not equipped for this as we only had our regular shoes and clothing. But, in spite of the snow on top, we made it and spent the night there in a hut where we were even fed. This was wonderful as we had run out of food altogether.

In 1950 my parents moved to Frankfurt and Ingrid and I followed as soon as the school year ended. Sigrid's parents moved there at the same time. What a lucky chance. We spent quite a bit of time together. One evening we listened to a speech given by German writer Heinrich Böll. Among other things he told us to travel to different countries and make friends with people there. He argued this would help prevent another war. We looked at each other and said: "let's go." We planned a trip to Switzerland, Italy and Austria and worked at getting passports and visas, which were still needed at the time. We also worked at odd jobs to earn some money.

As soon as the summer holidays started, we were on our way. We still had our old one-speed bikes, a tent and sleeping bags and what little else we needed. We loved Switzerland, with its beautiful blue lakes to swim in and the mountains. We also enjoyed crossing the Alps to Italy.

In those days there were hardly any cars on the road but a few trucks that seldom moved faster than 20 or 30 kilometres an hour. When the road got too steep, we waited for one of those trucks so we could grab onto it and hitch a ride up the hill. Once we were stopped by two policemen. But they were very friendly and just wanted to know where we came from and where we were going. At the end of the conversation they even stopped a truck for us to hang on. At night we usually put up our tent in a farmer's yard after getting permission to do so. Often we were invited into the house and even fed. We made many friends. We loved Italy, the people, the villages, the cities, the many wonderful buildings and art in Milan, Pisa and Rome. Often we had flat tires on our bikes and other problems, but somehow everything got solved. We rode on to Naples and then returned via the east coast of Italy. We stopped in Venice and had a great time there before returning home via Austria.

What a wonderful two months we had.

Since we planned to do a lot more travelling, we thought we'd better learn some languages first. In 1951 I had just finished a two-year teacher training program and Sigrid had finished high school. We decided to go to London as nannies to improve our English. I had to work harder than ever to look after three children and to do many household chores. After six months I quit and flew from London to Edinburgh, my first flight ever – I enjoyed it to the fullest. I then hitch-hiked through Scotland and Ireland, seeing lots of interesting places and meeting many friendly people. Back in London, I arrived just in time for the coronation of Queen Elizabeth. With Sigrid and thousands of Londoners, we spent the night in the street, singing and dancing, and then watched the queen and Prince Philip on their way to the coronation site and back again. Later the queen and her family stood on their balcony and waved to the crowd.

Back home in Frankfurt, I got a job as a kindergarten teacher and Sigrid worked in an office. Throughout the winter we planned our next move. This time we wanted to go to France to improve our French and to Spain to learn another language. We bought new bikes that had three speeds. I have never been so proud of any vehicle bought later as I was of this new three-speeder. In the spring of 1953 we left for France.

We rode north past Reims and Metz, visiting the beautiful Romanesque cathedrals, and into Normandy. The place we liked best there was Mont-Saint-Michel, with a huge cathedral on a tiny island. The water surrounding the place was even warm enough to swim in.

After a few weeks of travelling we finally made it to Paris. Since we were out of money by then, we got a job in a hotel as chambermaids. The work left us enough time to explore the city from one end to the other. The summer had just started when we left Paris and rode south, always camping and making lots of friends. In Marseille we took a boat to the island of Corsica and rode around this most beautiful place. Back in France, we spent three weeks working in wine country near the lovely city of Carcassonne, earning a bottle of wine each day besides our wages. In the evening we did a lot of partying with our fellow grape pickers, and one evening we cooked a meal of snails we had found on the vines. It wasn't my favourite meal, but it wasn't that bad.

By then fall was in full swing and we entered Spain with the idea of eventually continuing to the African continent. We were quite excited to see our first orange trees and climbed over the fence to collect some that had fallen off. Just then, two policemen on bicycles approached. They also climbed the fence and threw the oranges we had picked away. Then they climbed up the tree and picked the best oranges and gave them to us. Next they invited us to the village for coffee. We had a great time together in spite of language problems.

Just around Christmas, when we had arrived in Barcelona, we found a letter from Sigrid's mother, telling us to return home, as she was not well. She enclosed two railway tickets. What were we to do? We went home by train and spent a lovely Christmas with our families.

We each got a job and made the decision to travel away from Europe so we could not be easily called back. Sigrid had some relatives in Mexico, and she wrote to them to ask if we could visit. They said we could. That was the destination that eventually took us around the world.

CHAPTER 2

MEXICO, 1955–56

JULY 1955

Sigrid left for Mexico in June while I stayed back to attend the wedding of Ingrid (my only sister) to her fiancée Theo. Immediately after the ceremony, I boarded a ship to Amsterdam that would take me to Houston, Texas. From there I planned to fly to Mexico City. The ship was a brand new Dutch freighter called the *Wonosoba* that took along a few passengers. I liked the ship immediately. The cabins were nicely furnished, the showers and washrooms more than adequate and the dining room and reading room bright and pleasant. I shared my cabin with Heidi, an elderly lady who was on her way to Texas to keep house for an American family. She was very friendly but a prolific talker. There was also Mrs. Fonvielle, a delightful American lady, with her two young sons, Ricky and Skippy. Altogether we were eight passengers, and we shared our meals with the captain and the officers.

I enjoyed getting up early in the morning to watch the sky and clouds and the waves. I also liked to go out at night to see the light of the moon make a silver road on the water, or watch the stars that seemed closer and brighter than at home.

On August 5, the captain had his 50th birthday, and we all had a magnificent dinner and a great party. The next day was my birthday, my 23rd, and the captain brought me a small bowl made of the famous Dutch Delft china (I still possess it today). The steward arrived with a wonderful birthday cake and everyone else came with little gifts and congratulations. I felt quite touched; I thought nobody knew this was my birthday.

After about two weeks on board ship we had quite a storm, and anything that wasn't screwed down began moving. Luckily, the storm didn't last long, but it got very hot and humid outside. It was such a blessing that the ship had air conditioning. I wanted to read but was constantly interrupted by Heidi, who would tell the most uninteresting stories.

We passed close to Bermuda and, later, as we entered the Gulf of Mexico, we saw the lighthouses on the Florida coast. As we got closer to the USA mainland, we saw many dolphins swimming along the ship and pelicans flying by. We passed by Galveston, Texas, and shortly thereafter reached the Houston harbour. I found it hard to say goodbye to the *Wonosoba* and all the friends I had made on board ship.

At that time, Houston was a city of about 500,000 people, with huge buildings in the centre and many attractive parks. I spent the night in the YMCA. It was very hot and I did not sleep well. The next day I exchanged my plane ticket for a bus pass so I could see more of the country, and shortly afterwards I boarded a bus for Mexico. I liked the journey through Texas. Besides oil, cotton and cane sugar were the main products of the state. Everywhere, Black people were working in the cotton fields (just as we had read it as children, in *Uncle Tom's Cabin*, only the guards with their whips were missing).

Around midnight we arrived in Laredo, at the Mexican border, where the passengers had to cross a rickety footbridge over the Rio Grande. The proper bridge had been taken out by a flood. It was dark and still hot and there were bugs everywhere. I wondered what two more nights and a day on a Mexican bus would be like. The bus left Laredo at 2 a.m. The Mexican lady next to me wrapped her pesos in a sheet of newspaper and slipped them into her bra. I went to sleep, and when I woke up, the sky toward the east was bright red and the mountains to the west were covered in clouds with only the peaks showing. We stopped for a while in Monterrey, then left the fruit-rich flatlands and entered the mountains. Most people there lived in dirt houses and looked poor. The cities we passed: uninteresting. At every stop we were literally attacked by beggars and people trying to sell their wares.

The bus arrived in Mexico City the next morning. I found it chilly, then remembered the city has an elevation of over 2000 metres. I took a taxi to the house of Sigrid's relatives, the Priesemuths. They received me very kindly and both Sigrid and I were glad to be together again. Happily, we exchanged all our news.

After lunch, Sigrid's Aunt Priesemuth invited us to come with her to a village in the mountains where she wanted to buy some handicrafts. We went along and were amazed at the quality of workmanship produced there. We admired carved wooden objects, woven fabrics, embroidered garments and lace tablecloths. Inside the stone houses were many children and young mothers, either pregnant or carrying their infants. How did they find time to produce such beautiful work? From the outside, the houses looked drab, but entering the courtyards we saw flowers, bushes and trees. The rather empty rooms were accessed through arched doorways.

I liked Mexico City right away. The climate was wonderful, warm in the morning and hot in the afternoon. It rained almost every day (it was the rainy season), which helped to get rid of the dust and to lower the temperature. I met a lot of people through Sigrid and the Priesemuths but could barely communicate with them, so my first aim was to learn Spanish as fast as possible. On the weekend we made a trip to Aguascalientes, about 300 kilometres northwest of Mexico City. There were hot springs and we enjoyed a swim. Later we walked through the market and I was amazed at all the beautiful handicrafts. I think all Mexicans are artists! I loved the silver jewelry, the embroidery, the colourful handwoven textiles and the pottery in all shapes and sizes. Most men wore handwoven ponchos and the women big shawls called *rebozos*.

The food in Mexico was quite different. At first I didn't like the tortillas that were served at every meal and the black beans and avocados, but I soon acquired a taste for them. Aunt Priesemuth served wonderful meals and almost always there was a fruit or a vegetable or a combination of something that was completely new to us. The Priesemuths were very kind to us, and we tried to be of help by looking after their 2-year-old, Erika, and helping their 11-year-old, Carlitos, with homework. Carlitos attended the German school. Sigrid found a job as a substitute teacher at an American school. She had to teach Latin among other subjects, and since she didn't know any Latin, she always had to study ahead of her students. She also had to correct many tests that she was required to give. We spent many evenings correcting papers, which was my job, and learning Latin, which was Sigrid's.

I went for an interview at the German school and was told I could start as a German teacher after the main holidays on the first of February. In the meantime, I got a job teaching German to private students.

SEPTEMBER 1955

Sigrid and I found a place to live in the Calle de Tornel. It was a small place built on top of an apartment house. The Priesemuths gave us beds they didn't need anymore, plus a wardrobe, a table and two chairs. We made curtains, bought sheets and built a bookshelf and shelves for the kitchen. Our new home wasn't far from Chapultepec, the largest city park in Mexico. From our roof we had a great view of the city, and on clear days we saw the over 5000-metre-high volcanoes, Popocatépetl and Iztaccíhuatl.

The 16th and 17th of September were national holidays. We met two young German men, who decided to show us the Atlantic coast. We left around midnight and arrived in the small village of Tecolutla early in the morning. It was hot and sticky there, quite different from the cool mountain air of the capital. We swam in the ocean then put up a tarp and slept. The next day we drove along the coast and found a beautiful spot to swim. However, the ocean was quite rough. After we swam out a little way, the strong current made it hard to get back to shore. Later we went to a restaurant and ate a variety of fish. I found one dish very tasty. It was made from thousands of fish, each no bigger than the head of a pin. I also liked the hot spices (mostly chili) that made our mouths burn and brought tears to our eyes. Afterwards we sat together and talked and drank "made in Mexico" Moselle wine. We drove back to the capital, past coconut trees, banana plantations and fields of pineapple. We saw orange, lemon and grapefruit trees, as well as cactus and agave plants. From the latter, *pulque*, a pleasant, slightly alcoholic drink is made.

OCTOBER 1955

One weekend we took the bus to Teotihuacan, 50 kilometres northeast of the city. We had to hike quite a long time to get to the famous Toltec ruins in the Valle Misterioso. Once we reached it, we were impressed by the 70-metre-high Pyramid of the Sun, consisting of several pyramids, one on top of the other and erected at intervals of 52 years. On the highest plateau, human sacrifices were made to the gods. A little further away we climbed the smaller Pyramid of the Moon. We had a good view from the top of a green, hilly countryside. Between the two pyramids was a wide avenue, called the Street of the Dead, with many palaces and temples on both sides. In the main palace we admired the stone images of the feathered serpent, Quetzalcoatl, a god-king of ancient times.

There were an amazing number of buses in Mexico City with very skilful drivers, who not only managed to handle the traffic but also to collect fares at the same time. There were a surprising number of fleas on every bus as well. Our insect spray bottle became a much-used object.

I ended up finding a part-time job with a firm that did business with Germany; I had to handle their correspondence. I don't think I was too effective, since my typing skills were limited, as was my knowledge of Spanish. In the afternoon, I still taught German to Victor and Anina, the children of a Dutch couple. On Victor's birthday, 20 children were invited, and I had to use all my teaching and language skills (some spoke English, others Dutch, German or Spanish) to interest them in games and other fun things to do.

On the weekend we went to the theatre for the first time, then attended a divorce party (good wine was served there) and, finally, went to a dance. The cha-cha was the rage then. We looked on in utter amazement then joined the fun. We also hiked up the 4000-metre-high Pico del Águila with our new friends from a mountaineering club we'd joined. It was a good trip, but it rained as we came down and we all got thoroughly wet.

Another weekend we climbed the 5480-metre-high Popocatépetl. We had to get up shortly after midnight, and with our new mountaineering friends travelled in a rickety bus to the end of the road. From there it was a long climb. We saw little vegetation but lots of rocks. Later we reached snow. We felt the shortage of oxygen as we got higher and higher and moved slower and slower. When we reached 5000 metres, it began to snow, but we kept going. Only when the storm became really violent did we decide to turn back. We climbed down (five to a rope) and soon the snow turned into heavy rain. Once more we arrived home completely soaked and tired but happy.

The following Friday evening, we went to our mountaineering club to socialize and to sign up for a trip to the Iztaccíhuatl. This mountain rises up across from the Popocatépetl and is over 5000 metres high. We got up at three in the morning and started the hike just as the sun reached the snowy peaks of the Popo and Izta, turning them golden. It took eight hours to reach the top and we were all tired. On the peak we all embraced and congratulated each other and slapped each other's backs (that's the way it was done there). We had a beautiful view all around and then it was time to go back. As we descended, the pressure in my head diminished and I really started to enjoy myself.

We were so happy to have joined the mountaineers. They were such super people and we already had some special friends like Manolo, Marcello, Angel and Jaime. Our Spanish had also improved with constant use, and we were able to understand almost everything that was said and to join in conversations.

NOVEMBER 1955

One day we went to see *Porgy and Bess*, and the Negro Opera. Some of the melodies were simple, yet dramatic and moving. A few days later we went to see the play *La Otra Orilla*. It was about four people who died and lived on as ghosts watching their funeral ceremony and party. It was very funny.

One day our small window broke and I decided to replace it myself. I took careful measurement and bought a new glass. Unfortunately, the pane turned out to be slightly too small. This time Sigrid took the measurements and went to get the glass, but this time it turned out too big. Together we measured once more and bought the glass, which to our delight fitted perfectly. Shortly thereafter we came home on a rainy day and found the window open. Sigrid slammed it shut and the glass broke. Again we kitted a new windowpane into the frame. The same evening, coming home late, we realized we had forgotten our key. Luckily, the cement had not completely hardened yet and we were able to scrape it off, remove the window and get into our room. The next day we put in the window for the fifth – and, hopefully, last – time. I wrote a poem about this incident. Dear reader, how is your German?

> Als wir in unser Zimmer zogen ein
> Da musste auch eine Scheibe ins Fenster rein
> Denn eine fehlte.
>
> Ich nahm am Rahmen genau das Maß
> Und holte mir in der Stadt das Glass.
> Doch als ich es wollte setzen rein
> Sah ich, das Glas war zu klein.
> Sigrid sagte, Du bist aber schlau
> Und nahm das Maß nun ganz genau
> Und holte die Scheibe
>
> Nanu, was ist denn jetzt nur los,
> Die Scheibe ist ja viel zu groß.
> Nun gingen wir gemeinsam zum Glaser rein
> Und kauften die dritte Fensterscheibe ein.
> Und diese passte.
>
> Bald darauf kamen wir müde und nass nach Haus
> Und die Fenster standen beide auf.
> Sigrid schlug sie zu mit Macht
> Und da ist unsere Fensterscheibe zerbracht.

Die vierte Scheibe kauften wir ein
Und kitteten sie in den Rahmen rein.
Doch nicht für lange.

Am selben Abend gingen wir aus
Und als wir kamen spät nach Haus
Da merkten wir mit stillem Klagen
Das die Schlüssel vergessen imZimmer lagen.

Jetzt gab es nur zwei Wege, die Scheibe wegtun
Oder draußen im Freien ruhen
Wir taten das Erste
Wir nahmen den Kitt und die Scheibe weg
Und kletterten durchs Fenster und dann ins Bett.

Am anderen Tag kam die Scheibe zum 5. Mal rein
Und das wird hoffentlich das letzte Mal sein.
Wenn nicht folgt eine Fortsetzung.

We were still going out every weekend with our friends, who also taught us how to rock climb. It isn't as easy as hiking, but quite safe, as we were always roped and secured. We also learned to rappel, which was something I really enjoyed.

We celebrated Sigrid's birthday in a tent. We left home on a Saturday and camped near Pachuca, where most of our rock climbing took place. We took food and wine along and had a great party. The next day we did some serious climbing, at least our friends took it very seriously. The area around Pachuca is pretty. Between tall green fir trees huge rocks in all sizes and shapes rise toward the sky. Each one has a name. The people around the area were extremely poor as the land yielded little. Many lived in caves. There were a number of silver mines in the area, though not in use anymore.

In our street we were known as the *dos muchachas alemanas* (the two German girls). On the way to our bus stop, everyone – the baker, the shoemaker, the butcher and the mechanic – waved to us. Their stores were always wide open, as the doors were removed every morning and put in again in the evening. We felt quite at home in our neighbourhood.

DECEMBER 1955

We continued to work at our jobs during the week and hiked or climbed on the weekend. One time I went with Manolo and a few others to hike an especially difficult route up the Iztaccíhuatl. We left on Saturday afternoon and stopped at midnight to sleep under a tree. It was very cold at an elevation of close to 5000 metres, and then a storm began. First there was thunder and lightning, then rain and finally snow. Both Manolo and I had enough – we were cold and tired. We began the return trip and, after a few hours, found a cabin where we slept for a while in our wet clothes, sharing just one flimsy sleeping bag. When we woke up, the others in our group had arrived, telling us the storm had gotten worse, forcing them back.

The next weekend we went to Toluca, where we planned to hike in a canyon. This canyon was only 2–4 metres wide. A fast creek flowed within it, creating cascades and waterfalls. Slowly, we worked our way down the canyon, often falling into the water or getting caught in the downpour of a waterfall. It was a riot! The top of the canyon was covered with tropical plants that grew together, forming a light green roof over us and preventing the hot sun from getting through. After about two hours we reached the end of the canyon. From there the water fell straight down for about 50 metres. We could see our wild creek flowing peacefully along the valley bottom. We had planned to rappel down the waterfall, but our leader feared the force of the water would be too powerful, so we had no choice but to climb all the way up again. If the going down was hard, going up was even more difficult; we had to use rope on especially difficult sections. When we finally arrived at the top, we all sat in the hot sunshine until we were dry again.

We had a three-day holiday before Christmas and decided to take the bus to Oaxaca, 680 kilometres south. We enjoyed the trip through the mountains and the dry, hilly country further south. Except for three small towns, the area was largely unpopulated. The land was too dry for agriculture. Oaxaca is a delightful colonial town with impressive churches, marketplaces, old Spanish-style houses and charming hotels and restaurants. We listened to a lively marimba concert the first evening as we explored the town. The next day we hiked up Monte Albán to see the ruins of the Zapotecas, who began to build this place more than 2,000 years ago. We were the only visitors, and a friendly guide showed us around and told us about the history of the area. We admired the temples, underground passages, palaces, tombs, frescoes and statues of gods and animals.

As we walked down from Monte Albán, we met some people who invited us to come with them to Salina Cruz on the Pacific coast. It was quite a long trip, 300 kilometres over several mountain ranges. We stopped for a short time to admire the famous Tule Tree. The tree is supposed to be 2,000 years old, and it takes about 50 people with outstretched arms to encircle it. On the way to Salina Cruz, we saw iguanas, a coyote and a 1.5-metre-long snake. It was dark but still hot when we reached the Pacific, so we all went swimming. In the water were millions of little glowing insects like fireflies, and every wave or movement of arms or legs caused small fireworks. It was so unusual and so beautiful. When we got out of the water, our bathing suits and hair were still glowing. Later we walked around the town and admired the Salina Cruz girls, who all wore long, shift-like dresses. They were known to be the most beautiful girls in all of Mexico.

We got up early the next morning, had a typical breakfast of eggs, tortillas, fish and frijoles, and drove back to Oaxaca. We stopped en route to see the Mitla ruins. Mitla, a Zapotec settlement, was constructed around AD 100. It was the main Zapotec religious centre, dominated by high priests. The place was still in use when the Spaniards came to Mexico. We admired the beautiful stone mosaic style for which Mitla is so famous. There are 16 different mosaic patterns at Mitla, all geometrical and thought to symbolize the sky, the earth, the feathered serpent and others. Each little stone was cut to fit the design and then set in mortar on the walls and painted. It is estimated that over 100,000 pieces of stone were used on one building.

Back in Oaxaca, we went to visit the very ornamental cathedral and were duly impressed by the massive use of gold. We took the night bus back to the capital and arrived just in time for work.

For Christmas that year we decorated a small tree, went for a service at a German Protestant church, ate a special meal and opened our letters and parcels from home. On Christmas Day we sat in the sun on our roof and enjoyed a quiet day. On Boxing Day we both had to work, but in the evening we invited our Mexican friends over and had a party.

In Mexico, Christmas starts nine days earlier with a *posada*, which means "shelter." Friends meet every day in front of someone's house, light candles and ask to be let in. When this request is granted, a procession is formed and goes through the house, people singing and praying and looking for the crèche with Baby Jesus in it, which they will find beautifully decorated on the last day. After the procession, people eat and drink and play games. A favourite game is breaking the piñata, a decorated, candy-filled ceramic vessel.

JANUARY 1956

Following an old tradition, Sigrid and I wanted to spend the New Year in the snow, so we decided to climb Popocatépetl on our own. On Saturday afternoon we took the bus to Amecameca, hoping to get a ride from some mountaineers to Tlamacas, where the ascent begins. But no car came, and it took us seven hours until midnight before we reached the cabin at the trailhead. Five young men were already there, so we had to greet the New Year with them before crawling into our sleeping bags.

The young men got up at two in the morning and we followed at four. A full moon was up and the countryside with the two white volcanoes looked magical. It took us two hours to get to the *cruzes*, where snow covered the ground. We put on our crampons and hiked up the icy trail. Suddenly, the mountain peaks turned bright red and soon we were in the sunshine. It didn't get much warmer, though, as a cold wind was blowing. The climb got harder and harder, and it became more and more difficult to breathe. We were tempted to turn back but kept going and by 1 p.m. we were on top.

The view from the peak was worth the hard climb. We saw the almost-6000-metre-high Pico de Orizaba, the Iztaccíhuatl and other mountains and volcanoes all around us. We climbed down into the crater to get some protection from the icy wind, rested for an hour and started the climb down. This proved to be quite difficult – it was very icy and there was always the threat of falling. However, we made it, and we were also lucky enough to get a ride to Amecameca, where we took the bus home. Both Angel and Manolo came early the next morning to find out if we had arrived safely.

In Mexico, children get their Christmas presents on January 6, Three Kings Day, or Día de Los Reyes. In the evening, friends meet to cut up and eat a yeast cake called Rosca de Reyes. Inside the cake is a small doll symbolizing Jesus. Whoever finds this doll in his piece of cake has to give a dinner on February 3, another saint's day. We were invited to the Priesemuths', where we took part in the cake cutting. We were also each given a lovely hand-embroidered blouse.

FEBRUARY 1956

When we first arrived in Mexico, we each had a six-month visa, which were now running out. To get a new one, we had to leave the country. Consequently, we took two weeks off from our jobs and on the 14th of February left for Guatemala. We could have flown to Guatemala City but decided it would be more interesting to travel to the Caribbean coast in the Yucatán and take a fishing boat south to the coast of

Guatemala. (Little did we know!) Some Spanish friends picked us up to take us to the bus depot but at the last minute decided to drive us all the way to Vera Cruz. We arrived there early in the morning, had a refreshing swim and a good breakfast, and said goodbye to our Spaniards. Vera Cruz was a harbour town with a lovely white beach, quite clean and at that time with few high-rises. We took the bus from there to Coatzacoalcos, where we stayed in a small hotel.

Coatzacoalcos was the end of the road, but every morning a train left for Campeche in the Yucatán. The railroad had only been built two years previous, and it took 27 hours to travel through the swamps and jungles to Campeche. From there we hoped to get a bus to the Atlantic coast and a ship to Guatemala. We really enjoyed this leisurely train trip. Our fellow travellers were delightful, telling us about the country, and the animals in the jungle and insisting that we share their food. Whenever the train stopped, there were a few bamboo huts where some Indigenous people, descendants of the Mayas, lived.

It was very hot in Campeche. We visited a museum and an old castle and then took the bus to Uxmal, a famous Maya ruin. Uxmal is situated in the middle of the jungle. In order to reach the different buildings, we had to fight our way through high grass and brush. We were immensely impressed with the Pyramid of the Magician. It is oval, with 150 steps leading to the top, which is crowned with a small temple and decorated with masks of the rain god, Chac. We climbed up the steep, high steps and looked down on a green ocean of trees. We were truly surrounded by jungle. We followed a narrow trail that led to the Nunnery Quadrangle, decorated with dozens of long-nosed Chacmools (another name for Chac). Above the entrance of each building was a frieze showing warriors, kings and regular people. Next we admired the Governor's Palace, with its corbelled arches and rich frieze on the upper facade, and the House of Turtles. Finally, we went to see the House of Pigeons and the Ball Court, all wonderfully decorated. I found it almost magical to be alone with Sigrid in the jungle surrounded by beautiful structures that were built so many years ago then suddenly abandoned around the year 1200. What secrets must be hidden here! At sunset we reluctantly left Uxmal.

We travelled for several hours through the jungle until we reached Mérida, the capital of Yucatán. We took a horse-drawn taxi and went to a hotel, where we had a long-needed shower and a good rest. The next day we explored this delightful small town, went to the market and enjoyed watching the people. The Indigenous women all wore white cotton dresses that were beautifully embroidered and undergarments showing about 20 cm of lace. It looked very attractive. The men wore white cotton suits and big hats. We bought some oranges for lunch and fried tortillas filled with onions, beans, cheese and meat. We tried to get some information about the coast and ships to Guatemala but without success. Therefore, we left this delightful little town and continued travelling toward the coast.

The first place we came to was Chichén Itzá, another impressive Maya ruin. The most outstanding building there was El Castillo, a four-sided pyramid with 91 steps on each side. We climbed to the top and admired the flat jungle country below us. Then we walked to the Ball Court flanked by temples with beautiful stone carvings of gods, animals, flowers and trees. The Temple of the Skulls, the Temple of the Warrior and the House of the Thousand Columns impressed us deeply.

We admired the finely sculptured pillars, the reclining statue of Chac-mool and the stone-carved animal deities. Of immense interest was also the Sacred Cenote (well) where the Maya people sacrificed humans and precious objects to their gods.

We found it hard to leave Chichén Itzá, but our bus was departing and we had to go. The next town was called Valladolid, and we stopped there for the night. We met a bullfighter by the name of Manolo and spent a delightful evening with him and his friends. The hotel we stayed in had only hammocks in the rooms, but we found them quite comfortable.

We left Valladolid early in the morning by bus. The roads were unpaved and very rough. The other bus passengers were Indigenous people and chickens. Again we travelled through large areas of jungle. We saw the most beautiful orchids and other plants wound around trees, as well as many colourful birds. After five hours we reached Puerto Juárez, which consisted of only a few bamboo huts. We truly felt as if we had reached the end of the world. We walked to the ocean, which was green and clear and had beautiful white beaches. We found a fisherman who was willing to take us to the Isla de las Mujeres, a little island in the Caribbean Sea.

The tiny island turned out to be a real paradise. It was surrounded by white beaches and had the cleanest, clearest water we had ever seen anywhere. We could look into the water and see fish, turtles and shells in all sizes and colours. A fisherman rented us a bamboo hut, empty except for two hammocks, yet we were completely happy in our new home. We swam and explored and rested. Sigrid especially needed a lot of rest as she wasn't feeling too well.

We realized very quickly that trying to find a boat to Guatemala was quite unrealistic and decided to take the bus back to Mérida and a plane from there to Guatemala City. By now Sigrid had a high fever. As soon as we reached a hotel in Mérida, she went to bed. On the way to the pharmacy, where I hoped to get some medicine for Sigrid, I met Manolo, our bullfighter. He came with me and helped me arrange everything: a doctor, medicine, plane tickets, exit permits and whatever else we needed. He was just wonderful. Late in the afternoon, Sigrid felt better, and we all went to see the bulls Manolo was to fight the next day. We went out for dinner, met some people who remembered us from the train and we all had a good party. The next morning Manolo took us by car to the airport and off we went on a new adventure.

In Guatemala City, at that time a town of 150,000 inhabitants, we stopped at a cheap hotel. (The plane trip had made us quite poor.) We went immediately to the Mexican Embassy to apply for new six-month visas. We were shocked that we had to pay 11 quetzals for each visa (one quetzal equalled one American dollar). Now we really had barely any money left.

We found the Maya people in Guatemala even more colourful than the Mexican Indigenous people. The women wore handwoven long skirts, colourful cotton blouses, shawls and ribbons. The young girls all had ribbons braided into their hair. The men wore colourful pants, white shirts and sleeveless jackets. Some women carried their small babies in shawls on their backs, and a basket or jug on top of their heads. In the evening we listened to a marimba concert in the plaza. Twenty-four men played on eight instruments, and the sound was clear and rhythmic. Guatemala is the home of the marimba.

We would have liked to stay longer in Guatemala, but we had to get back to our jobs. We took a slow train to the border and enjoyed the leisurely trip. We passed by Lake Atitlán and a volcano by the same name. Both looked inviting, but we didn't stop. After 12 hours we reached the border. The visas were stamped, but we were asked by the customs officer to show that we had at least US$100, which we didn't have. He cancelled our visas and sent us back.

We were so astonished that we were left speechless. We sent a telegram to Sigrid's boss in Mexico to send us $200 and settled down to wait. We waited for three days in the tiny village with nothing to do. Luckily, the local police chief took an interest in us and invited us for a trip to the ocean. We drove in a Jeep through the jungle. The roads were impassable and covered with a foot of dust. Occasionally, we passed a couple of pigs. Just before we reached the ocean, the road ended. However, at this point several small rivers flowed together, so we hopped into a dugout canoe and were pushed along by an Indigenous man with a long pole. It was an exciting journey, especially after we were told that crocodiles lived in the river. We stopped in a village for tortillas and frijoles and fish – a nice change from our banana diet of the previous days.

On the fourth day our money still hadn't arrived, so we sent off another telegram. The next day an answer came back that the money had been sent to Guatemala City. We scraped our very last pennies together and Sigrid took the train to Guatemala City – a 24-hour ride. Three days later Sigrid came back. In the meantime, I almost died of boredom without books, without money and without food (except bananas, of course). Luckily, our friend the police chief took me out a few times. With our $200 we tried to cross the border again, but the customs officer still wouldn't let us across. We wondered why he disliked us so much. Was it because we didn't try to bribe him? If so, bribe him with what?

Just as we were wondering whether we'd spend the rest of our lives stuck between Guatemala and Mexico, another customs officer (a Guatemalan one) felt sorry for us and kindly suggested we try another border. He even offered to drive us. We said goodbye to all the kind people in the village and drove to the next town. After waiting for several hours for the right official (and with fear in our hearts), we got our visas stamped without trouble, and then we were back in Mexico. Two customs officers gave us a ride to Tapachula in a brand new car; we felt as if we'd escaped from prison! We had time for a swim before the train left. We rode north for 24 hours to Ixtepec then took the bus via Salina Cruz and Oaxaca for another 24 hours, and then we were home. All our friends greeted us with delight. Most of them had given up hope of ever seeing us again. Even we had wondered if we'd ever make it back! The principal of the German school was quite annoyed I had not shown up earlier, but obviously he needed me because he wanted me to sign a contract for four years. I refused and said I would not stay longer than six months. This annoyed him even more, but I still got the teaching position. Sigrid continued on at the German bookstore she'd found work at after quitting her job teaching Latin.

It took both of us more than two weeks to get over our Guatemalan journey. We were both ill, Sigrid more than I, and needed time to recover. Somehow we managed. I had to teach German to 32 preschool children – only four of them knew any German. Luckily, it was only for four hours a day. Besides, I really enjoyed it once I got used to the job. I was by far the youngest teacher in the school and often felt my colleagues didn't take me quite seriously. In the afternoon, I continued to give private lessons. The German school had an excellent reputation as one of the best in the capital. Around 2,500 children were enrolled from kindergarten to grade 12.

On the following weekend, I planned to go climbing with some friends. For some reason we didn't meet up. Not wanting to go back home, I took the bus to Amecameca and walked for many hours toward the mountains. It was cool in the shade of trees and I looked at flowers, watched animals and enjoyed being on my own. I spent the night in a small mountaineering hut and walked out the next day. At the house of an Indigenous family I stopped for huevos Mexicanos, scrambled eggs with lots of hot chili. By evening I was back home in the city.

MARCH 1956

With some Spanish friends, we made an excursion to Tequesquitengo. On the way we stopped in Cuernavaca, a delightful colonial town surrounded by a huge wall with beautiful gardens and parks. On weekend evenings, young people met in the plaza. There was the curious custom of young men walking in a circle in one direction and the girls in another. I imagine they eventually paired up!

We drove to Tequesquitengo Lake and rented a boat and water skis. We all tried water skiing for the first time. Sigrid learned the fastest! It was fun, especially since the water was refreshingly warm. Manolo was quite annoyed at us for playing tourists instead of going climbing or hiking.

At school a very important person from Germany arrived and everything had to be perfect. We also had a big teachers' dinner and dance and an all-day school party where every class performed for an audience. We preschool teachers had taught our students a Japanese kimono dance, which turned out amazingly well. The Mexican children looked delightful in their kimonos and all the parents were very proud.

One evening Sigrid and I went to an open-air performance of one of Vega's classical plays. On the weekend Salvadore, Manolo and I went to Pachuca, where we camped and climbed. A few days later, on a national holiday, we went with the Priesemuths to Tenampa to listen to a famous group of musicians. They wore black suits, embroidered with silver thread and silver buttons, and huge black hats. They sang typical Mexican songs and played all sorts of instruments.

It seemed that every weekend we were on the go, and sometimes in between as well. Mexico is blessed with many holidays, some national, others Catholic. We climbed rocks – El Zorro, Las Ventanas, El Corazon, Los Frailes, El Alcolito and others – all near Pachuca, a dry dusty area covered with thorny plants and cactuses. Both Sigrid and I got to like rock climbing, but we never advanced far enough to lead a climb. Rappelling on a rope down a rock face remained my favourite activity.

APRIL 1956

Sigrid decided to go to Acapulco for Easter, while I went with Manolo, Salvadore, Macello and a few others to climb all the peaks on the Iztaccíhuatl: La Cabeza, El Pecho, Las Rodillas and Los Pies. It was quite strenuous. I had trouble keeping up with the men near the top, but it was enjoyable all the same. As we were climbing down, one of my fellow climbers Manzanos suddenly got quite sick. He had to be led down and later transported back to the bus on a mule. He died a few days later and we were all terribly shocked. He wasn't even 30 and had a wife and two little children. We went with Manolo and our other mountaineering friends to the funeral. It was so sad.

Meanwhile, Sigrid and I started playing tennis in a club close to where we lived. We even had a trainer for a while who thought we had potential (he no doubt said that to everyone). Usually, we played early in the morning before school started and the bookstore opened.

One of the teachers at the German school asked me if I wanted to be her friend. Unsure what to say, I said "yes." Her name was Mummi. She was about ten years older than me, married and had three girls. Even though Mummi was born in Mexico (of German parents), she spoke excellent German. She was also quite artistic; she painted and did Scherenschnitte (scissor cut-outs). She invited me to her house quite often and I also met her parents and her brothers. One day she picked me up to drive to Las Estacas, an area rich in sugar cane. Las Estacas is a spring that quickly became a brook and a river. Plants grew in the clean water and little fish swam about. Mummi and I decided to swim the water from the source to a bridge about 20 kilometres away. It was the best thing we could have done on a hot summer day. We didn't really have to swim as the current pushed us along in the cool, clear water. However, we had to watch for impediments such as plants and tree trunks. We reached the bridge two and a half hours later, happy to have had such a wonderful day.

May 5 was another national holiday; Mexicans celebrated winning the Battle of Puebla against the French in 1862. Angel invited me to come with him, and friends Mario and Feu-Feu, on a three-day trip to the volcanoes. How could I refuse? We camped overnight in La Joya then started early in the morning to hike over all the peaks of the Izta, over 5000 metres high. I was in great shape and little bothered by the lack of oxygen. Suddenly, it began to snow and hail, then a moment later the sun came out, then we were covered in clouds. The sky offered a new surprise every few minutes.

On the peak, we tried to put up the tents, which proved a challenge. The wind howled and almost tore the tents out of our hands. We finally managed to put the two tents up. By that time I was so cold I thought I'd never be warm again. Angel massaged my feet and hands and I did the same for him. We crawled into the sleeping bags and tried to sleep. The altitude combined with the storm outside and the cold kept me awake. Luckily, the night passed, and then came the worst part: getting out of the warm sleeping bag and putting on my frozen boots and folding up the equipment. When we finally got down below the snow line, we stopped to prepare some food – we hadn't eaten in 24 hours. Then we slept for an hour before going all the way down and home.

On May 15 a week of school holidays started. I think I was more excited about it than the children! Sigrid, Irmgard (another teacher) and I decided to go to Acapulco since I'd never been there before. We started at midnight and arrived in Acapulco early in the morning. We went for a swim right away then found a nice hotel. I liked Acapulco, with its beautiful bays and tropical plants and flowers in abundance.

We stayed a few days, swam, went for a boat ride, watched a diver hurl himself over a cliff into a water hole and explored the city. On the way home we stopped in Taxco, one of the nicest towns in Mexico, with cobblestone streets, Spanish houses, a lovely cathedral and many shops selling silverware.

We were barely home when Manolo showed up and then shortly thereafter Jaime and Angel. We just started to party when Mummi arrived and insisted we all come to her house. We danced and sang there until midnight then went to our mountaineering club. There, everyone was in the process of going home, so the five of us went to a nightclub. The place was really weird, full of skeletons and skulls. The waiters were dressed up as monks and only a few candles lit up the place. A waiter monk showed us a collection of skeletons. Suddenly, one of the skeletons jumped at us. We screamed in terror and everyone laughed. While we sat at the table, huge spiders (plastic and on strings) came down from the ceiling and again freaked us out to the amusement of the other patrons.

The next day I went with Mummi and her parents to Tepoztlán, where they had a lovely hotel. Mummi showed me around. I was impressed with the beautiful mural she had painted. It told the story of a princess conceived by the wind, a legend of the area. We hiked up a steep trail to a small pyramid on a rocky outcrop. Legend has it virgins, only wearing flower garlands, were pushed down the rocks as a sacrifice to the gods. From our mountaintop we watched *águilas* (eagles) fly below us, as well as numerous *zopilotes* (vultures). I also noticed a bright red bug. Mummi told me that the red dye in this beetle was used to colour garments and clay vessels.

Tepoztlán was an especially pretty village. It had a monastery and a beautiful church and graveyard surrounded by a stone wall. The Indigenous people lived in small, whitewashed stone houses, with courtyards full of flowers, bushes and trees protected by stone walls.

JUNE–JULY 1956

During the next few weeks, we continued to do a lot of hiking and climbing because the rainy season was soon to start and that would be the end of our many outdoor adventures. Our year in Mexico was also coming to an end. We had to make up our minds whether to settle in Mexico (very tempting) or move on and see more of the world. We decided on the latter and applied for visas to the United States and Canada.

I spent a weekend hiking among the volcanoes all by myself and enjoyed the physical activity as well as the solitude. Also, we made up some rock-climbing parties to Pachuca and San Rafael and as always had a lot of fun.

Our mountaineering club put on a farewell party for us and we danced all night. Everyone tried to talk us into staying. Both Sigrid and I got several offers of marriage, but we definitely weren't ready for such a commitment. At the school, too, there was a party for me, and the Priesemuths and other friends held parties for us as well. We knew so many lovely people here and were really sad about having to leave. However, we were also excited about seeing new places and finding new adventures.

We heard the sad news that four of our mountaineering friends had died while climbing Mount Victoria in the Rocky Mountains of

Canada. We were all really upset and huddled together, trying to come to grips with this tragedy. Since we planned to go to Canada (for some reason, Sigrid didn't get a visa to the US), we were asked if we would take some memorial medals and place them on the mountain. To this we readily agreed.

Just before our departure, we made a trip to Tula, another one of the more important archaeological sites in Mexico. Tula was the main city of the Toltecs, who arrived there in the sixth century from the north. The Aztecs defeated them in the 12th century. Tula is best known for its stone statues of warriors that are over four metres high. They really were impressive, as was the temple of Quetzalcoatl, the stone jaguars and the Chacmools (rain gods). There were also a series of reliefs that showed the symbols of the Toltec warrior order: jaguars, coyotes and eagles.

We had one more meal with Manolo and another with Mummi, and then it was time to leave for Canada. A whole contingent of friends came with us to the airport for a last farewell and *abrazo* (hug). We both cried when we finally left Mexico behind us. It had been such an exciting and wonderful year.

Adios Mexico lindo y querido!

CHAPTER 3

CANADA, 1956–57

JULY 1956

We left Mexico City early in the morning and half a day later arrived in Windsor, Ontario. Around the airport the grass had been cut and the smell of fresh hay was delightful, so different from the smells in Mexico. We spent the night at the YWCA and in the morning started to hitchhike to Montreal. We enjoyed all the sparkling lakes and rivers, the green trees, the wild flowers and the neat country homes. One night we camped on the banks of Lake Erie, another next to the St. Lawrence River. We stopped to see Niagara Falls and were astonished at the amount of water that rushed down the falls with such force. We enjoyed getting sprayed by the fine mist. The people who gave us rides were all very friendly and almost all of them invited us for either a piece of pie or a hamburger. I remember wondering, "Is there anything else to eat in this country?"

In Montreal we went to see Gretel and Gerhard, friends from Frankfurt, and they helped us find a place to live. We settled into a one-bedroom apartment that was quite adequate for our needs. The following Sunday we all drove in Gretel and Gerhard's new Volkswagen to the Laurentians, a mountainous area north of Montreal. We sang a lot and swam in some of the many lakes that dotted the countryside. In the evening we went to a typical German beer party.

Once we were settled, we contacted Cove, a friend from Boston, and arranged to do the canoe trip we had planned when still in Germany. Cove promised to come to Montreal as soon as possible. To help pass the time, and to cut down on expenses, we got jobs as nannies and maids. This wasn't very exciting, but both our Canadian families were nice and we knew we wouldn't have to stay long.

AUGUST 1956

Our friend Cove arrived two weeks later, and we didn't waste any time quitting our jobs and getting out of the city. We drove northwest to the huge La Verendrye park, named after a 17th-century French explorer. We rented a canoe in Maniwaki, bought groceries for three weeks and continued driving on rough dirt roads until we reached the Ottawa River. It took a while to get all our equipment – tents, sleeping bags, food and clothes – stowed away in the canoe. Then our adventure really began.

It was quiet on the river and peaceful. We saw our first moose standing in the water. Even though we paddled so close that we could have touched it with our paddles, it didn't move. Later on we saw more moose, a variety of birds, squirrels and a weasel. None of these creatures seemed to be afraid of us. After a few hours of paddling, our shoulders and arms were hurting and we beached the canoe on an island. We climbed up a rock and found huge amounts of huckleberries, which we picked and ate while the mosquitoes feasted on us. We found a flat spot to put up our tent then tried to go for a walk. However, the bush was so dense that we didn't get very far.

The following day we left the wide river and entered a lake, where we camped on a sandy beach. We collected some wood and made a big fire, swam, cooked supper and even found time to get some "how to operate the canoe" lessons from Cove.

In the morning I was the first one to wake up. The sun was shining and I had a wonderful swim. When I got back, Cove had already lit the fire. We had breakfast and moved on. We left Lac Bouchette for the Camachigama River. It wasn't always easy to follow our map. The entrances and exits to and from lakes and rivers were often overgrown and we spent considerable time trying to find them. After lunch we reached two waterfalls around which we had to portage. Cove always carried the canoe and we made two trips each with our luggage. In the evening we found a beautiful flat rock on which we put up our tent. We again made a fire, and while Sigrid collected wild mushrooms and raspberries, Cove and I cooked an Irish stew. The wild mushrooms were terribly bitter and we had to throw them away, but the stew and the raspberries were delicious. After dinner we again practised operating the canoe: turning, stopping, going backward, forward, right and left.

The following day our river flowed into a small lake that didn't seem to have an outlet. We got out of the canoe and explored a narrow trail that eventually led us to a big lake. Obviously, we had to portage, which was hard work and took a long time. We were rewarded, though, because there was a logging camp, and the boss invited us for dinner and to stay the night. The food was unbelievably rich and plentiful and the loggers were great company.

After an enormous breakfast we continued our journey. Soon we came to two huge waterfalls and had to portage again. Here we found vast amounts of large huckleberries that we collected for dessert. Later Sigrid decided to do some fishing. She sat in the middle of the canoe and only Cove and I paddled. Even though she only had some string and a fairly primitive hook, Sigrid caught a fish within five minutes. Our very first fish ever! It was a northern pike and weighed about two kilograms. Then Sigrid caught another two. Cove showed us how to kill and clean the fish, and that night we had a feast. Unfortunately, it started to rain, and it rained all night and part of the next day.

We packed up the wet equipment and just kept paddling. In the evening we found an old abandoned log cabin and settled there for the night. It started raining again, and Cove got wet because the roof leaked where he was sleeping. It was still raining when we got up – we weren't too eager to get going. I took the canoe out for a while and caught my first fish, which I hated to kill. However, I did and we ate it for lunch. Then the sun came out for ten minutes and we packed up and paddled on. The sky was absolutely beautiful, blue one minute, black the next, then white, red, purple and blue again. It started to get dark when we paddled from the Capitachouane River into a lake whose surface looked like velvet. We put up camp, made a big fire and enjoyed being alive.

The next morning Sigrid caught another beautiful fish. Cove tried to get it off the hook, but it moved so much that it dropped out of his hand back into the water. He was quite annoyed. We thought it was funny. Soon afterwards we got into some fast water and really had to work to keep the canoe from capsizing. We then heard the roar of a waterfall and went up the bank to investigate. It was big enough to warrant a portage. Before travelling on we had a swim in the cold, fast water.

In the afternoon we found a great camping place next to a lake in an abandoned log cabin. This place was so ideal that we decided to stay there for two nights. I cleaned the cabin, Cove chopped wood and Sigrid picked huckleberries. (It was her favourite occupation.) Later I tried baking a cake by putting the batter into a pot with a lid and covering the whole thing with coals. It burned miserably! That night the stars came out. It was so beautiful that we slept around the fire.

The next day was Sunday and we hiked and fished and swam and relaxed. Monday started with a long and difficult portage that brought us to the big Camachigama Lake. We were in the middle of it when a storm came up. The waves became dangerously high, and we expected our canoe to tip. But we managed with great difficulty to reach the other side. The storm lasted all night.

Our supplies were getting low, so I made some bread out of flour, baking powder and water. I put the dough in a frying pan and baked first one side over hot coals and then the other. Everyone thought this was the best bread they'd ever eaten! (We must have been hungry.) Later we had to go up a fairly fast river, which would have been impossible had there not been bushes along the bank to help us pull the canoe along. It was a slow journey until we reached Indian Lake, which looked lovely with lots of little islands and tree-covered hills. From there we had to do another long portage. Only axe-cuts on some trees showed us the way. Our loads were heavy, the trail completely overgrown and the ground swampy. Clouds of mosquitoes followed us. Finally, we reached a small lake, where, completely exhausted, we put up our tent. The sunset was incredibly beautiful.

In the morning we fought our way up a hill through thick bush, hoping to orient ourselves. The forest was so dense that we couldn't see a thing. Cove climbed a tree and saw five different lakes in the distance, but they weren't where they should have been according to our map. We decided to return to the stormy lake. Tired, hungry, dirty and mosquito-bitten, we got there at the end of the day. Sigrid went out to catch some fish for us, Cove made a fire and I collected huckleberries. By now we had completely run out of food and lived off the land.

The next day, we found a small channel out of the lake and paddled all day. We were lucky to pass by another logging camp, where we asked if we could buy some food. The cook first fed us then prepared a huge bundle to take along. He absolutely refused to take money for it. We camped on a meadow next to a lake and watched moose, deer, ducks and geese pass by.

After that we paddled quite hard for two days, saw some moose and baked bread once more. In the late afternoon on the second day, we reached the place where we had left the car. Both Sigrid and I were quite amazed at Cove's ability to find the way back. Left to our own resources, I think we would still be in La Verendrye, eating fish and huckleberries. It had been a great trip. Sigrid and I couldn't thank

Cove enough for his friendship and guidance during this first wilderness experience in Canada. We drove back to Montreal, and Cove returned to Boston.

SEPTEMBER 1956

Instead of settling down and trying to find a job, we decided to see a little more of Canada first. We shouldered our packs and started to hitchhike west. Our first ride was with a French Canadian engineer. Near Mont-Laurier he drove off the main highway to show us a huge hydro plant. He took us around and explained how the system worked. The masses of water that fell way down into a river were almost as impressive as Niagara Falls.

We got our next lift from some French Canadian lumberjacks who were travelling to a logging camp to look for work. We camped in the evening and the following day were picked up in Smooth Rock Falls by the driver of a furniture van. He was in a hurry and practically drove day and night. The countryside didn't change much through Ontario. There were forests and lakes – and more forests and more lakes. The towns were quite small, often with just a few houses or even only a gas station and a bar or restaurant. Port Arthur and Port William, both wheat harbours on huge Lake Superior, were the first large cities after almost 1600 kilometres. Our truck driver let us sleep in the van, which was carrying quite a few chesterfields – we were amazingly comfortable for two nights. In Kenora, Ontario, at 5 a.m., we said goodbye to our friendly driver and marched at a fast clip along the road to get warm. Everything was covered with thick fog. But later the sun came through and it got warm, and we sang as we walked along.

We got another long ride and entered the Prairies. For three days we were driven through the provinces of Manitoba, Saskatchewan and most of Alberta. The prairies are quite flat, with huge wheat fields and big skies. The prairie towns seemed bigger and richer than the ones in Ontario. We found the city of Winnipeg quite attractive, with the Red and Assiniboine rivers flowing through it.

In Medicine Hat, Alberta – for the first time – we spent a night in a motel that was pleasant and inexpensive but very different from European hotels. When we got closer to Calgary, we saw huge grasslands with thousands of cattle and horses. That must have been the land of the buffalo before the white man eliminated them. Then we saw the Rocky Mountains, a huge chain on the western horizon.

We got a ride from somebody called Dave for the last stretch from Calgary to Banff. He was really neat. He showed us every landmark and knew the names of all the mountains. He was also the first one who knew of Mount Victoria and of our Mexican friends who had perished climbing the mountain. We told Dave of our plan to climb Mount Victoria and the promise we'd made to our Mexican mountaineering friends to deposit a memorial medal on the peak. Dave thought it was already too late in the season to climb it.

Dave also warned us about bears and advised us never to take food into the tent. To our immense surprise, we saw our first bear shortly thereafter, as well as moose and elk. We got more and more excited. The mountains became higher and more majestic the closer we got. We also saw beautiful turquoise-coloured lakes (the colour is so intense because of the limestone in the lake that is slowly dissolving), fast-moving creeks and beautiful forests.

We took leave from Dave in Banff, where he dropped us off at a trail leading to the youth hostel on the Spray River. By the time we got there, it was dark and the building was locked up. We walked around the hostel, found a partially broken window, climbed up and opened it from the inside. Sigrid started a fire in the stove while I collected firewood. We cooked some food and went to bed, grateful for a roof over our heads.

The sun was shining when we woke up. It was cold but lovely in the narrow creek valley. The Rocky Mountain peaks showed up beautifully against the blue sky. We walked back to Banff accompanied by squirrels. We also saw three grouse that barely moved as we approached. When we passed the impressive-looking Banff Springs Hotel, I had, of course, no idea that Felix, my future husband, was working there as a chief electrician.

In Banff we were sent to a Mr. Peren, a warden and mountain guide, to get a permit to climb Mount Victoria. He said it was already too late in the season and wouldn't give us one. Instead, he advised us to hike up from a place called Lake O'Hara to Abbot Pass, from where we would be really close to Mount Victoria. While we considered our next move, we hiked up Tunnel Mountain, a hill in the centre of Banff, from where we had a lovely view all around us.

The next day we got up early, cleaned up and left our youth hostel. Dave met us in Banff to show us more of the park. We stopped at one point and Dave showed us a hidden lake where beavers were busy swimming back and forth. We passed the controversially named Mount Eisenhower, which used to be named Castle Mountain due to its fortress-like appearance. (It had been renamed in 1946 in honour of the future US president's visit to Canada, but after decades of protest it was later re-renamed Castle Mountain in 1979.)

Dave told us so many stories that the time passed quickly. We drove up to Lake Louise, a beautiful green lake with the blue glaciers and the white snowfields of Mount Victoria in the background. Then we continued west until Dave dropped us off at Wapta Lake. From there we walked for two hours to reach Lake O'Hara. It was a beautiful hike. On one side was the steep rocky ridge of Mount Stevens, on the other the 3000-metre-high Cathedral Mountain. There was also Odaray Mountain with its glacier, Mount Wiwaxy, the backside of Mount Victoria and many others.

We came to small, green Lake O'Hara late in the afternoon and marched toward the log buildings. There, we met Charlotte, a 65-year-old energetic lady who was there to close up the place for the season. There was also Hedi Loehr, a friend from Banff, and Mr. Grassi, an elderly warden who was visiting. We were invited to join the group for tea. Charlotte insisted that, instead of camping, we sleep in the big guest house. We offered to help and she gave us chores to do, such as making up beds, chopping wood, setting the table and so on. In the shortest time, we felt quite at home.

In the evening Sigrid played the guitar and we sang. Charlotte came originally from East Prussia and Hedi from Berlin, so both enjoyed our German songs. There was a big fire in a gigantic fireplace, and we all felt wonderfully comfortable and content.

The next morning we helped Charlotte again with the chores then hiked up to Mount Wiwaxy. We saw Abbot Pass from there and decided to hike up and spend the night in the hut. Mr. Grassi lent us a rope and ice axes and gave us a permit to the hut. Charlotte filled our pack with food and even kindling to light a fire.

We started out in the early afternoon and hiked up and up. We reached three high plateaus, one after another. On the last one was Lake Oesa, a pretty green lake. From there we climbed straight up – it got steeper and steeper. We had been told it was only four hours to the hut, but the four hours had long passed and we were still climbing. It got dark, but we continued going because it was too cold to stop. Finally, we realized we'd lost our way and found a sheltered place in a kind of rock cave. We lit a small fire with the kindling we had and made some hot tea in my aluminum cup. The night seemed endless. At one time the moon came out and the mountain world from our rock cave looked awesome.

Finally, the night passed, the sky became light and it even looked as if the sun was going to shine. When we crawled out of our cave and looked down, we were absolutely amazed at what we had climbed during the night. We'd never have done it by daylight. We knew now that we were on the wrong route; Abbot Pass was below us and we were quite high up on the steepest side of Mount Victoria. It took us a long time (with the help of the rope) to get down. Charlotte and Old Grassi laughed when we told them our story, but they were also very nice and insisted we should come back and try again.

We were very tired and barely made it back to Banff, where Hedi Loehr expected us. Hedi was a delightful elderly lady. She came to Canada after her husband died in the Second World War and had brought along lovely pieces of art that were displayed in her house. We went to bed immediately but got up early to have breakfast with

Tante Hedi (as we called her). She had to go to work. The place didn't look very tidy, so we decided to do some housecleaning. We really worked hard; Sigrid even baked a cake and made coffee. When Tante Hedi came back, she enjoyed the coffee and cake with us but didn't appear to notice how clean the house looked.

The next day the sun was shining. Since it was Sunday, we went first to church and then hiked up Mount Norquay, one of the mountains around Banff. We had a lovely view from the top and were perfectly happy. On the way down we discovered 12 elk, among them an elk cow with two young ones. Later we met a bear, which permitted us to come quite close before disappearing into the forest. We walked on and, when we looked back, we noticed the bear had followed us but stopped when we stopped and stood on his hind legs. He had a white spot on his chest, which seemed to be itchy because he kept scratching it. The bear followed us all the way to the highway and only then returned to the forest.

The good weather held, so we decided to try Mount Victoria once again. We felt we owed it to our Mexican friends. We rented ice axes, hitchhiked to Wapta Lake and hiked into O'Hara. Charlotte seemed to be happy to see us. While Sigrid helped her with whatever there was to do, I decided to climb Yukness Mountain. It was already 3 p.m. and I had to hurry. I lost the path very quickly and climbed up on the rocks. Suddenly, I saw a ground squirrel (my first one) and I stopped. It came closer, smelled my boots and pulled on my laces. The evening on top of the mountain was absolutely magnificent. The sky was clear and the mountains and glaciers stood out perfectly against the darkening sky. When I looked over to Mount Victoria and saw what we had climbed a few nights ago, I was really scared. It was beginning to get dark – I had to get back. As I was running down the path, a full moon came up and everything looked even more magical than before. I met a small bear as I turned a corner. He was just as astonished as I was and disappeared quickly. I arrived back at O'Hara filled with joy about this wonderful afternoon and evening.

We decided to do our climb the next day and packed what we needed for two days on the mountain. We got up at 4 a.m. and started hiking by the light of the moon. We met a porcupine, which ran in front of us for the longest time before climbing a tree. This time we knew where we were going and reached the Abbot Pass hut after approximately four hours. In the hut diary we found the names of our Mexican friends on the first page. Four of them, all roped together, were killed as they came down the glacier. We wondered what we were doing here, with even less experience than they had. However, we took the ice axes, the rope and some chocolate and started climbing. It was not always easy, and we used the rope several times. At noon we reached the south peak. From there we had to go up a steep ridge to get to the main peak. Neither one of us liked this narrow sharp ridge covered with thin ice, but we tried it and, to our relief, made it. We buried the medal, said a prayer for our Mexican friends and started down, which was even harder than going up.

We reached the hut just before it got dark and were relieved and thankful we had achieved our goal. We cooked a quick meal and went to sleep. We were tired. Mount Victoria isn't quite 4000 metres high – a lot lower than the Popocatépetl and Iztaccíhuatl in Mexico – but definitely as challenging.

When we woke up it was snowing and the wind was blowing. How lucky we had been to have had a sunny day for our climb. We cleaned up the hut (Sigrid was a strong believer in leaving a place cleaner than she found it), and sang with gusto the Mexican national anthem, which the Mexicans had written into the book. Then we started to descend. By noon we were back at O'Hara. Charlotte and Old Grassi were happy about our successful expedition. We spent the rest of the day helping Charlotte fish.

The next day, after a good breakfast, we were given the job of blackening and polishing the stove in the main building, in addition to the ones in the log cabins. When we had finished we looked like chimney sweeps. After a shower we helped winterize the cabins before relaxing in front of the fire, eating, drinking and making music. It snowed during the night, and in the morning the valley looked absolutely beautiful. We helped Charlotte with some cooking and baking, and then Charlotte and I walked up to Odaray Pass. I was amazed at how well Charlotte hiked, in spite of being in her 60s. I hoped I'd be able to do that, too, when I became that old. The trail through the larch forest was very pretty. The needles had turned golden and the ones that had fallen looked like a carpet on the snow.

On the way back we passed by the Alpine Club cabin and met Hans Gmoser, a mountain guide from Austria, and Frank, a client from Montreal. Charlotte invited both for dinner and we all had a very pleasant evening. Both Sigrid and Hans played the guitar and we sang and talked. Frank worked for the summer in one of the hotels in Banff. Recently, he and his friend had gone climbing and both fell. His friend had been killed, but Frank barely received any scratches. To help overcome his fear of falling, Frank had engaged Hans to climb with him. The two young men invited us to go climbing with them the next day and we accepted with pleasure.

It was a beautiful sunny day, and Hans decided to go to Mount Schaffer. We found it a bit difficult to climb in the snow and ice but had so much fun together that we were on top before we knew it. We climbed down to the bright green Lake McArthur and walked to the alpine hut, where we made coffee and talked.

As much as we liked O'Hara, it was time to go. We said our good-byes to Charlotte, who loaded our packsacks with food, and to Old Grassi, who gave us each a mountain crystal. Just as we were standing by the roadside, trying to get a ride to Jasper, Hans and Frank drove up and attempted to talk us into coming to Banff with them, but we decided to continue our journey via Jasper. We got a ride with a friendly couple and together we drove through rain and snow showers over rough dirt roads. We didn't see much in the beginning, but when we reached the Columbia Icefield the sun came out, and we were impressed with the beauty of the mountain world around us. We found Jasper a pleasant little town and camped there for the night.

The next day we got a ride with two architects from Edmonton. They were quite funny, and we laughed and sang together. One of them insisted on taking us to the local TV station. They must have had pull there because when we arrived we were put on screen immediately and interviewed. We talked about our experiences in Mexico and our journey through Canada. Sigrid also played a Mexican song on the guitar and we sang "Voz de la Guitarra Mía." That was our first appearance on TV.

From Edmonton we hitchhiked to Regina, and the next day we travelled on to Winnipeg. We went to the YWCA to spend the night and came just in time to take part in a dance. We met scores of people, among them two young men from Frankfurt. We danced with them and later went out together and had lots of fun.

The driver who later took us to Kenora, Ontario, told us we could stay in his weekend house by the lake. We took him up on his offer and enjoyed a stay at our "own house." The countryside was quite beautiful; all the trees were in colour and the yellow of the birches, the reds of the maples and the greens of the conifers were mirrored in the blue water of the lake in the woods. We liked it there so much that we stayed an extra day and then leisurely moved on to North Bay and Ottawa. We were back in Montreal on October 4. We had seen a lot of Canada and met so many nice people that we actually looked forward to spending the winter in the country.

WINTER 1956–57

We found an attractive place to live on Pine Avenue, a quiet street with stately homes near McGill University in Montreal. Our room was pleasantly furnished and warm, our private bathroom spacious and the kitchen large and well equipped. Our landlady had bought the house and rented out the different rooms. Her name was Pearl. She was middle-aged, quite fat and liked to run around in sexy nylon nightgowns that left absolutely nothing to the imagination. After we'd been only a few days in the house, a man called and asked all sorts of questions about Pearl. When I couldn't give an answer to most of them, he whispered, "I warn you, you shouldn't stay in this house. I warn you." We heard later that Pearl was involved in smuggling narcotics but never found out if it was true.

Sigrid immediately found a job with Bell Telephone. I almost got a job as a teacher, but a Canadian also applied for the job and was better qualified. At a Jewish school I didn't get the job because I was German, and at a Protestant one I lost it because I was Catholic. Such is life! Then I found a job as a translator with CIBA, a pharmaceutical company from Switzerland. The job with CIBA was all right but a bit boring. Sigrid and I spent most of our weekends in the Laurentian Mountains, north of Montreal, first hiking and climbing, and later skiing.

We made friends with Roger and David, two students who lived in the same house and shared the kitchen with us. In the beginning they had trouble pronouncing our names, so they called us "Renaldo"and "Kelly." We didn't mind a bit and got used to those names. We also took in a little black cat that had adopted us.

For Thanksgiving, we received a nice letter from Cove's mother, inviting us to Boston for the long weekend. Unfortunately, we couldn't go, as we had to work on Monday. However, we were pleased Cove had thought of us.

In December it started to snow. We both found ourselves extra jobs at Eaton's. We worked Friday nights and Saturdays, Sigrid selling slippers and I, Christmas decorations. With the proceeds we aimed to buy ski equipment for ourselves.

One day Hans from Banff arrived, together with a young man from France called Philippe. (Both became life-long friends.) We invited them for dinner and stayed up into the early hours talking and laughing. We gave Hans and Philippe our room and took our sleeping bags into an empty one upstairs. Hans stayed for a week and at the end of it asked us if we wanted to come to Banff in March and cook for him and his guests in a ski hut in Yoho National Park. Needless to say, we were delighted and looked forward to that time.

On Christmas Eve we decorated a small tree with apples and candles, went to church, had dinner, and opened our parcels and read all our Christmas letters. The next day Pearl invited us all for a turkey dinner. Afterwards we walked with Roger and Dave to the top of Mount Royal. From there the city with its millions of lights looked very pretty. Later we would often walk up and skate with others on a snow-free little lake. Usually someone would build a fire, against which we could warm ourselves when it got too cold.

One weekend after Christmas we hitchhiked to Quebec City. It was a dull day and everything looked a bit sad and dirty. The St. Lawrence River was frozen except for a small area in the middle. People had built little shacks on the ice and were fishing. We liked the old town of Quebec, the Château Frontenac, the Citadel and many of the old houses. We got a room at the YWCA and went for another walk after dinner. It began to snow. A strong wind was blowing and we enjoyed being out. The trip home the next day was quite beautiful. New snow had covered the countryside and everything looked clean and sparkling.

With Philippe and his French friend, we spent a weekend in Sainte-Adèle to ski and another in Saint-Sauveur. After a heavy snowfall in February, we drove to Mont-Tremblant, the best skiing area in eastern Canada. By that time our skiing had improved somewhat and we enjoyed the long runs.

We quit our jobs in Montreal, packed up our few belongings and, in early March, began another journey west. We hitchhiked via Ottawa and North Bay to Sault Ste. Marie, crossed the US border and drove through Michigan, Wisconsin, Minnesota and Dakota. Near Winnipeg we came back into Canada, and it didn't take us long to reach Calgary and Banff. Camping in March was cold, but we managed.

In Hans's apartment in Banff, we found a letter from him telling us how to get to Little Yoho, and to get there as soon as possible. But we felt we needed a rest day. We went to visit Tante Hedi, bathed in the hot springs and walked around Banff. Hugo, a friend of Hans's, drove us to Field, BC, the next day, and the warden, as far into Yoho Park as the road was open.

We put on our skis, strapped our heavy backpacks on and started walking. Snow-covered mountains surrounded the narrow valley, and an ice-covered creek flowed beside the trail. We reached the halfway hut at Takakkaw Falls in the late afternoon. We made a fire and, since the hut was very dirty, we cleaned it from top to bottom. After dinner we lit a candle and sat around the wood stove, feeling that, after a long interval in Montreal, real life had begun again.

The next morning a marten stood on the snowbank in front of the window and watched us curiously. We packed up again and started the long hike to Little Yoho. The first three kilometres were relatively flat, but then the trail became steeper and we had to fasten skins to our skis to prevent us from slipping. After several hours of climbing, we reached the Stanley Mitchell Hut. Hans was glad to see us. He introduced us to his partner and friend Leo, also an Austrian. Hugo had already told us about Leo, saying, "Leo cuts wood, carries up supplies and kisses the girls." We also met Neil from Calgary, who came up almost every weekend to help and to ski. And then there were the paying guests: Mrs. Benfield and her three sons, Peter, Michael and David, from the eastern United States; and Don, Elsa and Fred from different parts of North America. We all became friends very quickly.

We started immediately to get the hut in order, scrubbing the wooden table and the benches and the kitchen counter, as well as all the shelves. Then we began cooking – everyone ate as if they'd been starving. The following day we baked bread for the first time in our lives, which, to our amazement, turned out absolutely delicious. We also made cake and cookies, and when people came back from skiing they were delighted with what we'd produced. (And here we'd been so worried about becoming cooks.)

The Stanley Mitchell Hut is situated in a small, snowed-in valley surrounded on three sides by evergreens and high mountains. The altitude is about 2000 metres. The hut has a small kitchen with a wood stove and a big living room with a fireplace and a potbelly stove, in addition to a small room called the boudoir where the ladies slept. The men slept in the open space under the roof.

Hans got up every morning at five and lit fires in all the stoves. As soon as they got warmed, Sigrid and I got up and started to prepare breakfast. We usually cooked dried fruit, porridge, pancakes, bacon and eggs. One of us did the cleaning up afterwards, while the other went skiing with Hans and the guests. For lunch we always made a soup and with it had bread or crackers, cheese, sardines, or whatever was available. For dinner there was always a lot of meat, canned vegetables, rice, noodles or packaged potatoes and, of course, dessert. The evenings were always pleasant. We sat around the fireplace, talked, joked, played the guitar, sang and had a great time.

At the end of the week, Hans and Leo took the guests back to Field. I decided to come along and help carry up supplies. I found the trip down the narrow steep trail very difficult and arrived considerably later than the rest of the group. Carrying a 30-pound pack on my back, it took four hours to get up again.

With the new guests we made wonderful trips every day, climbing up different mountains and passes. My favourite one was Mount Kerr, but the others – Emerald Pass, Mount McArthur, the President, the Vice President and Mount Pollinger – all came a close second. We loved skiing in the deep snow and improved slowly but steadily. For Easter we had a full house and were kept quite busy. Neil brought me the Easter egg colours I'd ordered and Sigrid and I coloured eggs. We made nests with Easter treats for everyone and hid them in the snow. The Easter egg hunt was a great success, as were the slalom races one sunny afternoon with prizes for the winners and losers.

Altogether we spent six glorious weeks in Little Yoho. However, like all good things, the time in Little Yoho came to an end and we all had to ski down to the world below. The further down we skied, the wetter and scarcer the snow became. By the time we reached Field, there was hardly any snow left. We were all extremely tanned and everyone stared at us or asked if we had been in Hawaii. In Banff we all went to the hot springs, and Leo joked that the water's colour would change after we'd all been through it. Sigrid and I stayed with Tante

Hedi overnight and then drove with Leo and Neil to Calgary, where Charlotte had arranged a party for us. Then Sigrid and I left for Alaska.

MAY 1957

As we travelled toward Alaska, somebody told us that the road there consisted of nothing but miles and miles and more miles. This was true to a certain extent. There certainly weren't too many villages or towns during the 3000-kilometre stretch between Edmonton and Fairbanks. For a long time we saw nothing but bush, once in a while interrupted by beautiful and wide river valleys. We passed three towns: Dawson Creek, which had some hotels and motels; Fort Nelson, with its wooden buildings and corrugated roofs; and Whitehorse, a larger city and army base.

The road to Alaska was unpaved and the dust that got through every crack in the car wasn't pleasant. We were covered in dust from head to toe in the shortest time. Even the cities didn't have paved roads. We hitched rides from all sorts of people: Indigenous people, prospectors, loggers, tourists and job seekers. Each one had an interesting tale to tell. An Indigenous Elder told us he lived in the area because he didn't like reserves, a prospector said oil and minerals found in the region made for a good living, and the loggers told us they earned twice as much up north as they did further south. They all admitted they drank too much because there wasn't much else to do.

From Dawson Creek northward we slowly entered a mountainous region. It became colder and there was still snow on both sides of the road. The 1400 kilometres to Whitehorse we rode with two Germans who were looking for work. We usually slept in one of the many government rest houses beside the road. They all had a table, a bench and a wood stove on which we could prepare our meals. When we arrived we always first looked for wood and kindling, lit a fire, cooked and enjoyed being in our own comfortable house. We never once had to share it with anyone. At night we spread out our air mattresses and sleeping bags and went to sleep.

On our journey we saw some eagles and other beautiful birds. What we didn't see was anything green. The landscape was still in the grip of winter and we longed for some grass and flowers, as the month of May had already begun.

We crossed the Alaska border and drove 320 kilometres inland to the passport control office. The customs officer checked our passports, but since we only had a transit visa, he refused to let us travel on. We were devastated. We had wanted to fly to Nome and hunt seals with the Inuit. We also wanted to hike around Mount McKinley (now re-renamed Denali). Now we had to go back 3000 kilometres just because we had the wrong kind of visa – it was disheartening.

We put up camp for the night and watched the northern lights illuminate the sky. Some appeared like wide bands of light that moved constantly, others took the form of spirals that turned, dissolved and reformed. The most amazing light display formed a landscape mirrored in a lake. It was truly amazing – and now we had to leave this fascinating place.

The next morning the first car stopped. A man named Maurice was in it. He had already heard about our misfortune and invited us to travel with him to California. That was a little further than we wanted to go, but we did travel with him as far as Vancouver. He was very friendly, so we invited him to stay with us overnight in the government hut. He even had an axe and was good at making fires, so we cooked and shared our meals with him.

After a few days we reached Dawson Creek and saw some spots of green grass and trees that were starting to show their leaves. We got terribly excited. The further south we went, the greener the landscape became. In Prince George we saw lilac bushes and trees in bloom, continuing all along the Fraser River. Spring had truly arrived. In Vancouver we had to say *adios* to Maurice. He was really a very sweet guy. He even asked me if I wanted to be his lawfully wedded wife, but I wasn't quite ready yet to become Mrs. Maurice.

We loved Vancouver at first sight. We liked the harbour and the mountains and the ocean with all the inlets. We also appreciated the cleanness of the city. We spent the night at the YWCA and the next day took a walk along the harbour. Some Japanese officers invited us to come and see their ship. On board we were served tea and laughed a lot as we tried to make conversation. As we were leaving, one of the officers asked if we had been to Japan before. When we said, "No," he asked, "Why not?"

Why not indeed.

We immediately went to the Japanese Consulate and were told we didn't need a visa for Japan. Then, terribly excited about this completely novel idea of travelling to Japan, we went from one shipping company to another, compared prices and settled on a freighter that left for Japan on the 29th of the month. It would cost us $200 each one-way.

With the tickets in our packs, and still two weeks to spare, we decided to go back to the Rockies. We got to Revelstoke, BC, and found the Big Bend Highway still closed. (At the time you couldn't travel in the winter by road from Calgary to Vancouver.) Since we didn't want to waste money on a train ticket, we decided to walk the 180 kilometres. It was a crazy idea because we'd have had to walk for a week. Luckily for us, on the second day a warden in a government car who wanted to check out the highway came along and gave us a ride to Golden. From there we travelled on to Banff and Calgary. Leo and Neil were quite surprised when we arrived and invited us to stay with them in their apartment. On the weekend we all went to Glacier, where Hans had another ski camp. On the train we met Adolf Bitterlich, another Austrian and a friend of Leo, Hans and Philippe, and we all had a lot of fun together.

The Glacier Ski Hut was not too far from the station. Hans, too, was quite astonished to see us, but welcomed us with open arms. We all went to bed early because we had to get up at three in the morning in order to ski before the snow got too soft. Hans got up even earlier, made a fire and then Sigrid and I cooked breakfast. It was still dark when we got going on our skis; only the very tips of the mountains had turned a golden colour. It was a long ascent through wild country. There were innumerable creeks in full flow. We saw signs of bears, rabbits and wolverines everywhere. We hiked up the Asulkan Pass and had a ten-kilometre-long marvelous ski down.

We were back at the hut around noon and everyone went for a snooze. In the evening more people arrived, among them Bruno Engler, whom we had met in Banff, and Pat, Carol and Jean, whom we knew from skiing in Little Yoho. It was good that we had prepared a big meal! After dinner Hans played the zither and we danced and sang.

The next day, when we were skiing alongside a creek, we saw a wolverine on the other side. It hadn't heard us because of the noise the tumbling waters made, so we were able to get a good look at this ferocious, rarely seen animal. We stayed with Hans until the end of the week and did the most amazing ski tours in the most spectacular country. Then it was time again to leave.

Since we still had five days before going to Vancouver, we decided to make a trip to Mount Assiniboine, a mountain shaped like the Matterhorn and often called the Matterhorn of the Rockies. We packed food for four days, plus sleeping bags, a tent and skis, and started to march. We didn't know the area but had a map to follow. After several hours we reached Brewster Creek and followed the narrow creek valley. Steep grey rock walls rose above us on both sides. In the afternoon it started to rain, but we kept going in spite of the weight of packs and skis. Finally, we came to a hut and stopped there for the night.

I got up at four in the morning the next day, made a fire and woke up Sigrid. It was a beautiful morning, with blue sky and new snow. We had to cross a pass but couldn't find the trail, as all the tracks were covered with new snow. We finally put our skis on and just went up. At one point I slipped and fell into a creek. Sigrid, instead of being sympathetic, just laughed. The going got really tough, especially since we weren't sure where we were going. For a while we took the skis off again, and even though we often sank deep into the snow, it was easier to get around trees, rocks, creeks and other impediments. Finally, we reached the Assiniboine Pass, from the top of which we saw our mountain for the first time. It was so beautiful that it was worth all the pain it had taken to get there. It took another couple of hours before we reached the Assiniboine hut and the frozen lake in front of it. The cabin was open, so we made a fire, got some water from the creek and made some tea. Too tired to cook (we had been going for 12 hours on each of the past two days), we crept into our sleeping bags and slept.

I woke up at four in the morning and stood in front of the hut, admiring the beautiful peak and hoping to climb it one day. It was very cold and the snow was frozen hard. We decided to leave the skis behind and hiked on the still-hard snow over the pass. Later it got warmer and we again sank deep into the snow, but still we made much better time than the day before. We used a different route back via Bryant Creek. Everywhere we saw tracks of elk, moose and bears. Around noon we reached Spray Lake, which was still partly covered with ice. We followed the Spray Creek until it got dark. We made a fire and went to sleep. We didn't even bother to put up the tent. We were too tired.

We got up at 4 a.m. again and felt as if we hadn't slept at all, but we did enjoy the first few hours of hiking. At one point we saw a mother moose and her newborn. When she saw us, she climbed up a steep slope, but the little one had trouble following on its wobbly legs. Very quietly we moved away.

We reached Banff in the late evening. The first person we met there was Hans, who invited us for dinner. Sigrid didn't feel well and went to bed, staying there most of the next day. I visited with many of our Banff friends, such as Elsa, Charlotte and Tante Hedi. In the evening Sigrid felt better and we drove with Hans to Calgary. We had a wonderful party with Hans, Leo and Neil, and then it was time to leave. It was hard. The last three months had been absolutely wonderful, and the friends we had made had become so dear to us. That is the tragic part of travelling; you have to say *adios* too often.

From Calgary we hitchhiked south through Idaho, and then west through Washington and north again to Vancouver. We arrived in time to board our ship to Japan.

CHAPTER 4

JAPAN, 1957

We still found it hard to believe – we were on board a ship on our way to Japan. We left Vancouver on a beautiful summer morning and sailed south to Seattle, where the ship docked a full day. It happened to be Memorial Day in the US, and together with a friendly man we watched a military parade on the main street. Our man then showed us around Seattle and invited us for a meal in the elegant officers' dining room. From there we had a beautiful view over the green bay and the blue ocean. Everything looked and smelled of sunshine and summer. After our long winter in the mountains, and in the Canadian north, this still appeared miraculous to us.

As our ship was ready to leave the harbour, everyone on board held onto colourful paper ribbons that connected them to the people standing on the dock. A Japanese girl threw us some ribbons and waved and laughed. We also waved and laughed and felt part of this colourful scene. As the ship pulled away, hundreds of paper ribbons moved in the wind and looked absolutely charming.

From Seattle our freighter cruised first in a northwesterly direction, past Vancouver Island, the Queen Charlottes (now named Haida Gwaii), southern Alaska, the Aleutian Islands and then west toward Japan. Since we left Seattle the weather had been rather cold and miserable. The ship carried approximately a hundred passengers, about half its capacity. They were divided into three classes: the first class, whose passengers we rarely saw; the second class, which was occupied mostly by missionaries; and the third class, which was almost exclusively Japanese, except for a passenger from India, a quiet Australian lady, a Chinese gentleman and Sigrid and me. The name of the Indian man was Jaiswal. Everyone called him Mr. India or Mr. Peace Maker. He was travelling around the world to spread Gandhi's message of peace. At that point he had already travelled 85,000 miles. Jeffrey Joe was from China, and we found him very pleasant. The Australian lady never said a word and kept very much to herself.

Our steward was very funny. Whenever he wanted to tell us something, he did it first in Japanese, then again in Japanese with a few English words thrown in. If we still had no clue what he was saying, he just laughed and laughed until we couldn't help but laugh with him. Sigrid and I had a nice four-bed cabin to ourselves on the between deck.

Our food on the ship wasn't exactly what we were used to, and there never seemed to be quite enough of it. And then there were the chopsticks. On the first day we just sat there and were amazed how fast the Japanese ate their rice and fish and whatever else there was. We had barely started when they were finished already. But we learned quickly and soon we could use the chopsticks almost as fast as the Japanese. The food always arrived in five or six little dishes for each person. There was always rice and fish, a vegetable and two or three things we couldn't identify. Some stuff tasted really strange to us. One night we had octopus for dinner, cut into small strips. To us it tasted like sauerkraut made of rubber, but our Japanese friends loved it. We also found the Japanese food very colourful: red ginger, dark-green seaweed, light-green noodles, bright-red carrots. I believe the cooks dyed everything before they served it. Some nice young people shared the table with us and we often exchanged foods. With tea, we sometimes had cake, but more often mashed sweet brown beans in one form or another.

After the meals we usually walked around the deck between all the masts, ladders and ropes to get some exercise. In the evening we often watched a Japanese movie or danced. Once, we played bingo and I won three towels. A lot of our time was spent learning Japanese. We had bought a book, *Japanese in a Hurry*, and were trying to learn, but it wasn't easy. Fortunately, our Japanese friends helped us, especially with the pronunciation.

We had a communal bathtub on the ship, almost like a tiny swimming pool. We first had to wash ourselves outside the tub, then rinse the soap off with buckets of water and then soak in the tub. This was all rather pleasant. We were told that, in Japan, men and women use the same tub.

On Sundays the missionaries in second class always invited us to their service. One of them preached, another one read from the bible and we all sang and prayed with gusto. Their favourite song was "What a Friend We Have in Jesus." After the service we were invited for tea, had a friendly chat and returned quite happily to our friends in third class.

One day everyone got very excited when some whales were sighted. And, indeed, it was a wonderful experience to see these huge animals swiftly gliding past our ship. Later the weather finally turned, the sun came out and it was so much nicer to be up on deck. When the sun set, the whole horizon was coloured red and gold. At night we saw algae light up the waves (apparently, they have phosphorus inside their primitive cells). It was quite a spectacle.

After three weeks on board the *Hikawa Maru*, we finally saw land: Japan. At night we watched hundreds of brightly lit flashing boats, whose beak-like prows moved up and down in the waves. Everything was so beautiful and strange. Then, on June 14, we docked in Yokohama. Before we had a chance to leave the ship, we were interviewed and had some pictures taken by a lady reporter who, for some strange reason, was interested in us. The next day our picture and story appeared in a Tokyo newspaper and several people stopped us in the street to ask if we were the German girls the paper had written about.

One of the missionaries on the ship, a Miss Flowers, took us to a friend's place. They knew of a mission in Tokyo where we could stay for a few nights rather inexpensively, and after a meal were even kind enough to drive us there.

It took us a while to get used to Tokyo, then a city of eight million. Everything was so noisy there, and so different. If only we could read the signs! But we did enjoy ourselves. On the first day, as we explored Tokyo, we met a young Japanese who showed us all sorts of temples and parks and then insisted on inviting us to a theatre where we had no clue as to what was happening. The next day was also spent wandering about the city, but in the evening we met 12 of our friends from the ship and went for dinner to a Chinese restaurant. We then sat in a cafe and heard Mozart, Beethoven and Schubert, which reminded us of home.

As we didn't want to stay forever in Tokyo, we decided to buy bicycles and travel north to Hokkaido. Unfortunately, we found the Japanese bikes quite expensive, about US$150. Just as we decided to buy used ones, we met two American soldiers who took us to the PX store, where we got brand new German bikes for only US$75 each. These bikes even had three gears, lights, luggage racks and stands. Needless to say, we were delighted.

When we left Tokyo on our bikes, it was as if we had started again from where we had stopped a few years ago in Portugal. We both felt extremely happy to be free and independent again. Unfortunately, the paved roads stopped as soon as we were out of Tokyo, the weather was hot and damp and it rained quite often. The roads were simply terrible and consisted of more holes than dirt. Many of these holes were filled with rocks and stones, which made cycling even harder. We had a flat tire almost every day and became quite proficient at fixing them. Going downhill was no joy either because we had to brake like mad to keep the bikes from falling apart. The relatively few cars that overtook us enveloped us in a cloud of dust, so that by evening we were dirty, our eyes red and swollen from the grit. We became a bit apprehensive about bicycling in Japan. But after the first five days we more or less became used to being on the roads again, even on poor unpaved ones. We put up our tent every evening and had no trouble finding spots with access to water. When it rained, it was quite cool during the night, but when it was hot and humid during the day, the temperature changed little overnight. There were also quite a few mosquitoes.

We visited Nikko, a tourist town north of Tokyo, and were impressed by the beauty of the landscape: the mountains, Lake Kasumigaura, the Nantai volcano and the Kegon Waterfall. We were also impressed by the famous Buddhist temple complex begun in the eighth century (when Buddhism first reached Japan), with its beautiful detailed woodcarvings – one of them a sleeping cat. It was so lovely and peaceful there that we could easily understand the popular Japanese saying, "Do not say *kikko* [splendid], until you have seen Nikko." We also saw an enormous gilded Buddha statue. Priests in white robes burnt incense in front of it and young girls danced.

We left the main road after we'd passed the city of Sendai and bicycled north along the east coast. The mountainous roads were so narrow that whenever a car approached us we all had to stop and then carefully navigate past each other. Luckily, there weren't too many cars as most people travelled by train.

The Japanese are very friendly people. In areas where not too many strangers strayed, we were often invited into the house. We quickly learned to take off our shoes at the entrance and to put on the slippers that were provided. These were also left behind as we stepped on the mats in the living room. The whole house, except the bathroom, kitchen and hall, was covered with these straw mats. Then we sat or knelt with our hosts on cushions around a low table, drank Japanese green tea made on a small charcoal fire nearby, ate some Japanese goodies and tried to converse in our very limited Japanese. Except for the low table, there was no furniture in the rooms. At night, mats and bedding were taken out of built-in closets and in the morning returned there. Thus, the rooms, completely bare of clutter, always looked tidy. The inside walls were made of thin wood frames and covered with paper. We found it hard to imagine a bunch of rowdy children in a Japanese house.

Most people wore modern clothes in the cities, but in the country almost everyone was dressed in kimonos or long and wide farmer's pants and roomy jackets. Practically all men and women wore wooden shoes. These consisted of a flat sole with pieces of wood under the heel and toe. Strips of cloth and leather between the toes kept these shoes, called *getas*, on the feet.

Everywhere farmers were busy with sickles, cutting unripe-looking grain and hanging it up in bundles over poles and fences, presumably to dry. Others were planting rice seedlings in the muddy ground. Everything was done by hand and with great care.

The villages looked very charming, but often there seemed barely enough room for them between the ocean and the steep, tree-covered mountains. Of the cities along the east coast of northern Honshu, we especially liked Matsushima, situated in a beautiful bay, as well as Ishinomaki, Kesennuma, Taneishi, Miyako and Kuji. All were leaning against mountains and looked over bays, rocky islands and the ocean, with fishing boats and other vessels. Each place was full of life and colour. We spent days pushing our bikes up the hills through sparsely populated areas then down again on the other side. It was tough but rewarding. We were especially fascinated by the many rocky islands in the sea, some of them so small that only a few pine trees grew on them. We loved all the cuckoos, of which there must have been millions, and the frogs in the rice fields, whose concerts put us to sleep every night.

Whenever we stopped in a village to do some shopping, the local people always came to look at us. They'd bow and smile and we'd do the same in return. They were also interested in our German bikes and were always delighted when we told them we were made in Germany too. Sometimes half the villagers came and watched us putting up our tent. But everyone was polite at all times, bowing when coming and bowing when addressing a person or when going.

Once we met a young lady along the roadside by the name of Keiko, who was 28 years old. (The Japanese always asked, "What is your name and how old are you?") She insisted that we come to her house. We had tea there and baked goods filled with sweet soya beans and later rice, vegetables and an egg. We talked and talked, helped along by sign language. Later Sigrid played her guitar and Keiko made music on a harmonium (a small type of reed organ). We took leave from each other with regret on both sides.

Another day we spent in the house of Koko and his wife Sashiko. They were the sweetest people and couldn't do enough for us. First they prepared a steam bath for us. When we were finished, and wore the kimonos they had laid out for us, we sat down for a lovely meal of rice and curry. Then, as always when we stayed longer than half an hour at one place, a reporter came to take pictures and ask questions. Our hosts were delighted, and we tried to be especially nice just to please them. Koko and Sashiko insisted we spend the night with them, and in the evening the mats were put on the floor and everyone went to sleep. When we woke up the next morning, Koko had already left for work and Sashiko accompanied us to the end of the village. When we said our goodbyes, she started to cry. We were very touched by this.

We learned very soon that when we asked someone for directions, the person almost always jumped on his bike and took us where we wanted to go. If they didn't know, or didn't understand us, they usually brought us to the only white people living in the town or village, who were usually delighted to see us and wanted us to stay with them. It wasn't always easy getting away.

Once, on a narrow road in the mountains, we met Father Heidrich, a German monk. He had a lovely round belly and nice round cheeks. When he heard we were from Germany, he laughed with delight for at least five minutes, saying over and over again, "No, this is not possible: German girls! I haven't seen any German girls for 15 years, nor have I spoken German." He absolutely insisted we come with him to a convent, where a number of female Trappists lived. (Trappists take a vow of silence; except for prayers, they never speak.) Father Heidrich was their spiritual guide. He lived outside the convent walls together with a Japanese monk, who assisted the nuns with work in the fields. Sigrid and I were installed in a small hut. Father Heidrich, the monk and one of the nuns who was specially assigned for us did everything in their power to make life for us as pleasant as possible. When it rained the next morning, Father Heidrich brought us some rubber boots, the little nun umbrellas and the monk an electric heater to keep us warm. When it was time to leave, tears were streaming down Father Heidrich's cheeks. We were near to tears ourselves.

A few days later we met a French priest who stopped when passing us with his Jeep. After chatting for a while, he said he wanted to show us his school for children with intellectual disabilities that he had established and managed together with some Japanese nuns. We followed him and he gave us a tour of the place. We were deeply moved when we saw the 60 children who were cared for with love and affection. When it was time to say *sayonara*, one sister handed each of us a hand-painted bookmark and another a snack for the road.

We were also quite impressed with a lady Baptist who had lived in Japan for 30 years. She had established a school, a hospital and a farm, and strongly believed in her god and her ability to convert "the heathens."

Once we stopped at an orphanage and entertained the children with songs and stories. Everyone had fun, and the sister who ran the place also enjoyed the change of routine. She couldn't do enough to spoil us.

We noticed, as we travelled along, that the nicest and biggest building in each town or village was the school, and each one had a large playground. The children all wore uniforms, the girls a kind of sailor's outfit, with a blouse and a skirt, while the boys wore clothes our fathers would have worn 40 years previous. We visited quite a few schools, usually by invitation from teachers we met. We admired the children's discipline and eagerness to learn. Everyone worked as hard as possible to be among the few who would make it to college and university. In a small village we stopped to take part in a Sports Day. The children displayed their athletic prowess, while mothers in pretty kimonos danced and some old men organized relay races. We had a wonderful time being part of this special school day.

One evening, just as we had put up our tent, cooked and ate our rice and vegetables, and were ready to hop into our sleeping bags, two 18-year-old girls stopped by for a visit. They were curious and enthusiastic, so we built a fire, made tea, talked and sang German, English and Japanese songs. The girls were so impressed by this strange adventure that they didn't want to leave. When they eventually did, we heard, as we often had before, "We will never forget you." I thought to myself, "Nor will we!"

One night, after we were already asleep, I was awakened by men's voices. Worrying about the bikes, I sat up, wondering what to do, when some hands touched the outside of the tent. Before I knew what was going on, a hand poked inside through a gap in the tent's entrance. "What's the matter?" asked Sigrid, just then waking up. "Someone's hand is inside the tent," I said. "What shall we do?" Sigrid said, "Bite it." So that's what I did. Without even thinking about it, I grabbed the hand and bit into it as hard as I could. There was an enormous scream in the darkness. Whoever was there disappeared, and we went back to sleep peacefully until the next morning.

We finally reached Aomori, at the most northern point of the island of Honshu. We went to the house of Miss Flowers, a missionary we had met on the boat who had invited us to stay with her. It was good to have a few days of rest, to write letters, wash clothes, put a new seat on my rather worn-out pants, mend the tent and clean and perform maintenance on the bicycles. It was also good to reflect on the past three weeks in Japan, which so far had been quite amazing. We had met so many people, saw so many places and experienced so much that was new to us in this "Land of the Rising Sun."

Through Miss Flowers we met quite a few other missionaries and even took part in a few prayer meetings. We learned a lot about their work and their hopes and dreams. Of course, they all wanted to convert the "pagans," which apparently wasn't easy. Once a young person became a Christian, it was hard for him or her to find a Christian mate – no serious Japanese Christian would marry a non-Christian. Parents also strongly opposed the conversion of their children to Christianity. Who would worship the ancestors if their children didn't believe in the old religion anymore? In many houses, though, people had added a cross to their Buddhist and Shinto shrines. One more religious symbol – one more god – couldn't do any harm, and might have even been a benefit.

Among the many missionaries we met, we generally liked the Catholics the best. They spent most of their energies building schools and hospitals and teaching by example. The Protestants, on the other hand, seemed more fanatic, more bent on preaching, or at least on combining good deeds with preaching. However, we did feel sorry for many of the single women alone at some outpost, with little contact with the outside world. We also felt sorry for the missionary couples that had to give up their children as soon as they were old enough to go to school in order to be educated in their home country.

We boarded the ferry from the main island of Honshu to the island of Hokkaido and had a rough, four-hour sea journey from Aomori to Hakodate. We liked Hakodate immediately. It is a big city between two oceans, the Sea of Japan and the Pacific, and two mountains. As soon as our bikes were unloaded, we rode to Matomachi 21, an address given to us in Tokyo by the German Embassy. Here we found Carl Raymond, a German sausage manufacturer, his Japanese wife, and Linda, their adopted daughter. They all appeared absolutely delighted to see us and told us they'd hoped to meet us after they'd read about us in the papers. It seemed that all Europeans or North Americans in out of the way places were starved for non-Japanese company. The Raymonds did everything they could to make our stay pleasant, and after the first half-hour we had to promise to stay at least for a week. Before we knew it, they had made up a program to cover the next few days.

Mr. Raymond – he insisted we call him Papa – had two passions: food and politics. Since he liked food so much, he believed we did too and heaped our plates during mealtimes and in between, whether we liked it or not. Then he spent hours talking to us about a united Europe, world peace and the part he played in trying to achieve these goals. Both Sigrid and I had learned to listen. We realized many of the people we'd met hadn't seen a European for a long time and needed to talk.

Mrs. Raymond – now our Mama – was short and stout and absolutely sweet. Linda had come to the Raymonds from Germany in 1938 as a governess for their only daughter, Fanny, who was studying in Tokyo at the moment. Linda was 38 years old now and had never been back, as both her parents and one brother had died during the war. Furthermore, the Raymonds didn't want her to go back. She was terribly shy and afraid of so many things. I think she was the happiest that we were there – she spent hours talking to us about her life in Japan and her modest dreams for the future.

We spent one day helping Papa in his salami factory, where the finished products were sold to foreign ships, watched Mama in the kitchen cooking up the most delicious dishes and went with Linda to a tea ceremony. Another day we took part in a flower-decorating lesson, went swimming in the ocean with Papa and met Mama's lady friends at a tea party. One morning was spent typing letters to world leaders, in which Papa explained his ideas in detail as to how the world could be made a better place. We also gave the usual interviews to newspapers and radio stations. Two journalists took us in their car to the highest mountain in the area, where we had a splendid view over the city, the Pacific Ocean and the Sea of Japan.

Shortly after the papers came out with our pictures and stories, we had a call from a young man suffering from tuberculosis, asking us to visit him in the sanatorium in Sapporo. We also had a call from a German lady in the interior, married to a Japanese man for many years, who wanted us to stop by. We told both callers we'd be delighted to do so.

We were actually quite eager to keep moving on, but whenever we said we wanted to leave everyone got so upset that we kept postponing it. Actually, this holiday from travelling was rather nice for us, except we were getting too spoiled. One day Papa noticed our patched-up pants and immediately called a tailor to have some new ones made.

"Our" house in Hakodate was situated between a Buddhist temple and a Catholic church. The old Catholic priest had his 60th birthday and all of us went to the church to congratulate him and celebrate. Afterwards Linda took us to the Buddhist temple and then to her Japanese teacher's house, where she had learned the old Japanese art of drawing with white sand. The white sand is thrown on a black lacquered surface and divided up into the most beautiful designs. We liked the teacher's house. Instead of paper on the sliding doors, she had them covered with split bamboo, which went well with the mats on the floor. Except for a flower arrangement in the corner, and a low table and a charcoal fire with a teakettle, the room was empty.

We were also invited to a solemn tea ceremony. We half-knelt, half-sat on the floor (which was hard on our legs) and watched the tea being prepared. Every movement was prescribed. Then, one after another, we were given a fairly large bowl with thick green tea that we had to drink slowly (and also with the right movements) in three and a half gulps. I found the tea terribly bitter.

We finally managed to leave the Raymonds with our pockets full of salami and other delicious food and many good wishes for a speedy return. Like the rest of Japan, Hokkaido is very mountainous. Few people lived there when we visited, as the climate is too severe and unsuitable for the cultivation of rice, the main staple of the Japanese diet. Those who moved to Hokkaido at that time were almost considered pioneers. Although many people came there to stay after the war, Hokkaido was still less populated than the rest of Japan. Many of its forests had never been cut, and we were told some bears still roamed in them. An Indigenous group, the Ainu, who are the original inhabitants of Hokkaido, also live there. Their ancestors once lived over much of northern Asia, but in modern times their numbers have been greatly reduced. Many Ainu had also intermarried with Japanese settlers. The Ainu used to live in separate villages near the sea, where they hunted and fished. We met quite a few Ainu people as we biked in Hokkaido.

We bicycled overland straight north to the famous Lake Toya, next to a lovely volcano, and then on to the Noboribetsu Hot Springs. Hot steam was rising everywhere, and the muddy ground was blowing up big bubbles. On the following day we reached the ocean again and the Golden Route, a 150–200-kilometre stretch of highway around Uchi-ura Bay. It was called the Golden Route not because it was so incredibly beautiful but because it was so expensive to maintain; enormous waves crash over it at all times. There were huge holes in the road and many parts of it were missing where the rough sea had undermined it. We were amazed that buses still dared to use this highway. There wasn't much room between the rocky cliffs and the sea, but wherever there was a tiny spot, there was a house and a fishing boat. The fishermen were all busy drying *kombu*, a seaweed rich in vitamins and used as a vegetable. The weed, several metres long and about 30 centimetres wide, was dried on the pebbly beach and then cut and packed into bundles.

In the late afternoon the fishermen took their baths outside their houses in huge cauldrons with small fires underneath, which the children fed constantly to keep the water at an even temperature. We watched the men (they were always the first to have their turn) climb into the tub, relax there or climb out and take a stroll to cool off – all stark naked. They were most amazed to see us pedalling by and waving happily. We left the ocean near Biro and began pushing our bikes into the mountains. On the way we met an American Mennonite missionary who invited us into his house. It was a beautiful, new, European-style house. It even had a shower, and for the first time in Japan we enjoyed this luxury. His wife and children were also very friendly and said over and over again how much they enjoyed meeting English-speaking people. They pressed us to stay for a few days, but we moved on the next morning. After pushing the bikes for a long time, we reached Lake Akan and two volcanoes, Me-Akan and Cacan.

We were quite amazed to find a campground there. After we'd put up our tent and completed our chores, some young men asked us to join their group. There were about 25 of them. They had built a huge fire and were singing, clapping and dancing. We joined in the fun. It was a beautiful night and we all enjoyed being together. In the morning the rain came down in buckets and never stopped all day. The young men accompanied us to the end of the village, gave us each a kerchief as a farewell gift and sang "Auld Lang Syne" in Japanese as we started to bike off.

We spent hours pushing our bikes up and then riding down the muddy roads and up and down again. The roads were extremely narrow, and whenever a bus passed we had to get off the bikes and lean into the rocks. We passed one bus whose two wheels hung over a precipice and we wondered how it would ever be moved from there.

In the late afternoon, tired, hungry and wet, we reached a small village where we bought some vegetables and bread. The shopkeeper insisted we stop and dry out a bit and then served us hot cocoa.

Feeling a lot better, we biked on, reaching Lake Hangetsu and on the following day the small town of Kitami. From there we had to cross another mountain range. We put up our tent right on the pass, where the air was fresh and clean and the view magnificent. Wherever we looked were forested hills and also some snow-covered peaks. At night the sky was ablaze with stars and we said once again, "If people knew how wonderful it is to travel around the world, they would all join us."

The descent the next day was long and really enjoyable. On one side of us was a roaring mountain creek, on the other steep cliffs with many waterfalls. By noon we reached flat country. It was uncomfortably hot and there was a lot of traffic and dust. We stopped near Asahikawa, where we met a nice young man who told us he had watched American movies every day for five years and thus learned English. He wanted to show us the nearby Ainu village but took us first to a hotel that belonged to one of his relatives. Similar to homes, Japanese hotels also had no furniture except a low table and a clothes rack. In the evening, the *tatamis*, thin mattresses, were put on the floor and picked up again in the morning. We were served tea and the usual bean-filled baked cookies Papa had called bear droppings. Then we had a much-needed bath.

After we visited the Ainu, we went to a cafe and afterwards to a bar, where our young man was terribly worried that the one glass of gin we had would get us dead drunk. We then visited a Japanese wine house, where we had sake and dried nuts and where everyone looked at us as if we'd just come from Mars. Well, we rose to the occasion – Sigrid played the guitar and we sang some songs. Other people started singing too and the place became quite lively. Before we left, the barkeeper presented us each with a lovely fan. Our friend gave us lacquered chopsticks in a wooden container to remember him by.

We reached Sapporo, the capital of Hokkaido, on a sunny Sunday. We were told by almost everyone we met that the second-best beer in the world was produced there. We tried it and liked it but lacked the taste buds to appreciate its superior quality. We were looking for a campground and someone suggested the big garden of some German nuns. We went there and the eight sisters were delighted to see us. They hadn't met any Germans for a long time and asked us if we knew the places they came from (which we did), or any of their relatives (which we did not). They hadn't been back home – as they called it – for 25–30 years. Usually, nuns get a holiday after 10–15 years, but the war came in between and after that they couldn't go because there was so much to do and not enough staff to do it.

These nuns had founded a kindergarten, an elementary school, a high school and a college. Altogether they had 2,500 children enrolled, many of whom boarded with them. In each class were 80 children and there was a waiting list. We again were amazed how disciplined and eager the children were. A sister told us that, during recess, children lined up to recite to their teachers what they had learned by heart. If there wasn't time for them to have a turn, they would hand in pieces of paper with their memorized poems or stories written down.

The Mother Superior insisted we stay at least a day, and the nuns made a plan for us: breakfast at 8 a.m., bath at 8:30, school visit at 9:00, drive to the university with a nun and the French teacher at

10:00, lunch at 12:30. At 1:00 p.m. two students arrived to show us the town. With them we spent part of the afternoon visiting the sanatorium where the young man lived who had phoned us in Hakodate. He was very happy to see us and so were the other tuberculosis patients. Soon the room was full and we sat and talked and answered questions. Someone produced a guitar and Sigrid played some songs and others made music too. As we left our friend gave us a poem he had written, and he and the other patients all stood on the hill, waving goodbye. In the evening a sister took us to the university, where she taught an English conversation course. The students were given permission to ask questions about our travels and the two hours passed very quickly. When we finally got to bed, we were more tired than after bicycling 100 kilometres on dirt roads, but we felt we had won many friends.

When we left Sapporo on our way to Otaru, we couldn't believe our eyes: there was a 37-kilometre-long paved road. It was pure pleasure to pedal up and down the hills without having to worry about holes in the road, rocks and dust. But the pleasure didn't last long. After Otaru, we left the coast of the Sea of Japan and bicycled to Kutchan, where we visited two lady missionaries, friends of Miss Flowers. One of them was Irish, the other Australian, and it didn't take them long to figure out that not only the pagans needed salvation but Sigrid and I also. Oh boy, did we ever get a sermon! At the end of it they each prayed loudly for us, which took forever. I didn't dare to look at Sigrid for fear of doing something inappropriate. Those missionaries were great people, and I thought it was wonderful the way they believed in their god – but why did they have to be so obtrusive?

Renate

Sigrid

Rock climbing in Mexico.

Rappelling from the top of "La Botella."

Renate with her friend Angel.

Renate on a sunny day on a mountaintop with friends.

On the summit of Popocatépetl (5426 m or 17,802 feet) in the summer of 1956.

TOP AND BOTTOM Climbing on Popocatépetl.

TOP Renate's climbing companions.
BOTTOM Renate rests after a strenuous but beautiful day.

TOP The Stanley Mitchell Hut in the Little Yoho Valley of British Columbia, Canada.

BOTTOM In Glacier National Park in western Canada.

Sigrid on her way to Mount Assiniboine in May 1957.

Sigrid on her way to Mount Assiniboine.

Erling Strom's Halfway Hut on the way to Mount Assiniboine.

TOP Sigrid and Renate with their bicycles in Japan.
BOTTOM Renate and Sigrid with a group of young children in Japan.

TOP Renate and Sigrid visiting the home of Yamasaki-San.
BOTTOM Visiting the Missawa family.

99

Sigrid and Renate in Hokkaido.

Visiting with the Shozo family in Haroizuma.

TOP A newspaper clipping from the Sault Ste. Marie newspaper from March 19, 1957.
BOTTOM A newspaper clipping from a Japanese newspaper showing the girls on their bicycles.

東海道の松並木を快走するヒックさん（左）と ヒルテ さん 「自転車にくらべると ずっと楽」とご満悦である

A photograph from a Japanese newspaper showing the girls on their new motor scooters.

Sigrid and Renate repairing their bicycles in Japan. Due to the un-paved and neglected roads in the country the girls were constantly working on their bikes.

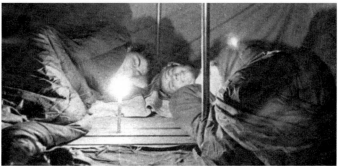

TOP The girls with their new motor scooters.
BOTTOM The girls in their little tent. Most of the time Sigrid and Renate camped.

TOP The girls gassing up their motor scooters in India.
BOTTOM A beautiful woman in Nepal.

TOP A celebration in
Kathmandu.

BOTTOM Sepp Dubach, the
Swiss cheese maker, carries his
skis in the Lang Tang region of
the Nepalese Himalayas. In the
upper left of the photo you can
see Mount Everest.

TOP Inside a house in the mountains of Nepal.
BOTTOM Sepp Dubach surrounded by his Nepalese friends.

An elephant in India.

On Scooters in fog.

Fixing scooter in India.

TOP Ferrying the motor scooters across the Ganges River.
BOTTOM Women working on road construction in India.

TOP Below the great pyramids in Giza, Egypt.
BOTTOM Men along the roadside near Assyut in Egypt.

TOP The Blue Mosque in Istanbul.
BOTTOM At the Lion Gate in Mycenae, Greece.

TOP Renate and Sigrid in Bulgaria.

BOTTOM Sigrid and Renate tour the sights of Sofia, Bulgaria, with their new friends Entscho and Ivan.

After three years of travel, Renate and Sigrid arrive back in Frankfurt.

Kutchan lies between two mountain ranges, and we were told it has so much snow in the winter that two-storey houses can be buried. The next day meant crossing one mountain range after another. It was also very hot and humid, so we got quite tired and soaking wet from perspiration. As usual we also had a flat tire, which didn't help to improve our day. Finally, we reached the Pacific again. There was a light breeze and a lovely beach. We had a refreshing swim and, feeling strong again, cycled on.

In one village a parade was in progress. Huge masks and decorative heads were carried about, the children wore festive costumes and all had a long white mark painted on their noses. Men made music on all kinds of different instruments, and in front of some houses rice was sprinkled. We couldn't find out what was going on. Everywhere fish were drying on racks and the smell was quite overpowering.

It was quite late when we came to the house of Mrs. Missawa, the German lady who had phoned us in Hakodate. She had already read in the papers that we were close by and was expecting us. The Missawas were quite a family. Mrs. Missawa had married her Japanese husband 30 years earlier, bore him five children and helped to work his farm. Tragically, her husband had drowned two years previous, when the big ferry from the mainland sank in a storm. His only son, then 21, became the boss and, together with his two sisters, ran the farm. Two other sisters married, one of them to an American. The children made all the decisions, employed people and looked after the money. Mrs. Missawa got an allowance every month, and if she needed anything extra, like clothes, the children bought them for her. Mrs. Missawa was quite funny and energetic. Her children didn't speak German because their father hadn't wanted them to. They also ate only Japanese food. Thus, we had fish soup for breakfast. I still remember it because I thought it was so awful (whole fish heads were floating around in the bowl). Even though the father was a Christian, meals were served to his spirit three times a day and placed on a mantel right next to his picture.

The following day two French priests we had met on the road invited us for dinner. We were delighted. We ate a fantastic French meal with them and shared two bottles of wine. Mrs. Missawa came far too early to pick us up for a movie, of which we understood very little. Then we stopped at a cafe, where we were introduced to many of Madame Missawa's friends and then went back to the farm.

We left the following day. As we bicycled along we reflected on the past weeks. We both decided that it was the people who had made this trip so wonderful: the owners of the bicycle shops who oiled our bikes for us or pumped our tires and tightened the screws; the people who gave us water to drink; the strangers who invited us into their houses; a couple who had passed us in a car and then waited on top of a mountain for us to serve us lemonade. There were many others and they all made our trip more special. Unfortunately, we had also suffered some losses. One of our fully loaded bicycles fell on top of the guitar and crushed it, and we lost our only camera.

Back in Hakodate we were received like long-lost friends. Fanny, the only child of the Raymonds, had arrived and we quickly became friends. She was a pretty 19-year-old and the only one who could stand up to Papa. The four of us went swimming every day, and one weekend we took the train to the foot of the Komagatake volcano, which was still active. We climbed over the hard lava and had to rest often since neither Linda nor Fanny was in good physical condition. From the top we looked into several craters from which the smoke belched into the sky. When we came down we walked to Lake Onuma, swam, picnicked and took the train back home again.

AUGUST 1957

My birthday on August 6 became a reason to celebrate. Everyone brought presents and Linda made a birthday cake. Sigrid gave me a kimono, Mama a pretty tray, Linda a sake set and Papa material for a blouse, plus a voucher for a tailor to sew it. Sigrid also got presents in advance because she wouldn't be there in November. We were once more very touched by the kindness and generosity of the Raymonds.

One day we went with Linda to the temple where Mama's family was buried. A friendly Buddhist priest showed us around. In the main room was a huge Buddha and a big drum. The walls and ceilings were beautifully carved. In another room, we were told, were 1,500 statues of Buddha and other deities. We didn't count them, but there were many. The third room was dedicated to the god of the sea, an important god in Hakodate, where most people depended for their livelihood on the ocean. The priest then showed us the prayer cloths that were folded like fans and when moved back and forth looked quite pretty. Finally, he let us each choose a stick, on which a piece of paper was fastened, that told us our fortune. Linda read it for us and we were happy to know that a lot of good luck was in store for us!

The days in Hakodate passed very quickly. We really wanted to leave, but everyone put up such a fuss whenever we mentioned the subject that we delayed our trip day after day. One evening I got a bit tired of the constant company and went for a long walk by myself. It was dark when I turned back, and a heavy fog was rising. Suddenly, all the houses and streets looked the same to me. I was lost. I took a taxi back and everyone thought this was absolutely hilarious. They never let me forget it.

One day we were invited to a professor's house. He and his wife took us to a restaurant where we all sat on the floor around a low table. A young girl brought in hot coals and placed them in a special metal container built into the table. Water was boiled over the coals, and vegetables and meat and noodles were cooked right there. Everyone then fished whatever they liked out of the pot, dipped it into little individual bowls of soya or radish sauce and ate it. It was very good. We were often asked out to formal meals by friends of the Raymonds and more informal ones by friends of Linda or Fanny. It was important to always ask Papa's permission; otherwise he flew into a rage or wouldn't let us go. In spite of his generosity and many other good qualities, he was quite a tyrant. We admired Mama, who cheerfully put up with all his whims.

When we applied for and received a new visa for another three months in Japan, and had taken our bikes completely apart and put them back together again so they were as good as new, we were ready to leave. Again our packs were filled with provisions. We were also handed 60 stamped and addressed postcards, so we could write to Papa and Mama every day. To top it off we were given train tickets from Aomori to Tokyo. We were quite speechless at the amount of generosity shown and found it hard to say goodbye.

We had a good ferry trip across to the mainland. We said hello to Miss Flowers and told her about some of our adventures and gave her greetings from the missionary friends we had visited who wanted to save us. We spent one more night in Aomori and then boarded the train to Tokyo.

The train ride was quite interesting. Everyone felt quite at home, took off their shoes and tucked their legs under or stretched them out. When it got hot, women took their blouses off and folded up their kimonos and the men rolled up their pants. The west coast of Japan was just as beautiful as the east coast. The Sea of Japan was bright blue and the coast very rocky. There were thousands of islands, some so small only one or two trees grew on them. In one area we saw lots of wooden containers floating on the water. Every once in a while a head and an arm showed up and something was thrown into the container. We were told what we saw were women diving for pearls. We were amazed at how long they managed to stay under water before coming up for air.

Back in Tokyo we were delighted by all the mail that had accumulated. We found a letter from Fuji Industries, a motor scooter firm, offering us a motor scooter for the remainder of our time in Japan in return for some advertising. We were absolutely amazed. It didn't take us long to think the proposition over and get in touch with the company. Mr. Matsui, one of the representatives from the firm, was very nice. The first thing he arranged for us was to take a driver's test, since neither of us had a driver's licence.

This proved to be quite a challenge, as it took us forever to find the place. An even greater challenge was to find an English translation of the Japanese traffic rules. The best part of the day was already over when a harried employee finally produced one. We were given half an hour to study the rules and then complete the written test. This must either have been satisfactory or nobody could decipher what we had written, because we were invited to come back the following day with our scooters to do the practical part of the driving test. We phoned Mr. Matsui, who said two mechanics on scooters would pick us up the next morning. They did and drove us to the park where they showed us how the scooters worked. Then they hopped on the back seats and we drove through the Tokyo traffic. We must have been rather odd-looking pairs with our Japanese mechanics sitting behind us on the scooters, because many people stopped and waved or laughed. We passed the test with flying colours (I think they were just happy to get rid of us). Then our men took off with the scooters, and we walked to the next subway.

On the way we saw a cafe named Heidelberg. Since we were hungry, we walked in and were greeted like long-lost friends and wined and dined by the owner, a Mrs. Heidelberg as we called her. She was a German who was once married to a Turkish man and lived with him and his other two wives. When she had had enough of this, she married a Japanese man who owned coal mines in China. He lost his life, and the coal mines followed, after the war. She settled in Tokyo and made her living with the cafe and restaurant. She called a reporter while we were there, and we did some advertising for her by telling him how excellent the food was (which was very true). We finally managed to get away.

The next few days were very busy ones. We appeared on a TV show where the audience had to guess who we were, which didn't take them long. We also had to get passport pictures taken and go to the Indian Embassy to get a visa for India, our next destination. This was a rather pleasant place, and we were invited there for a cocktail party. We also had to visit several shipping companies to find a freighter to take us to India in a month or two. All this took plenty of time as we bicycled from place to place, and not one of them was easy to find.

We met two Japanese men who spent seven months scootering from Calcutta (now Kolkata) to Paris. We also spent a delightful evening with the two Americans who had helped us buy our bikes when we first arrived in Tokyo.

Between all this running around, we found time to phone a Japanese judge. My Uncle Karl had given us his address, only he had misspelled it as "Fudge," so that is what we called him. Our Fudge, who sounded very nice on the phone and spoke excellent English, invited us to spend a day in the country. He took us first to Kamakura to see the huge statue of the seated and meditating Buddha surrounded by impressive temples. This Buddha had sat there in the open for over 800 years – neither fire, earthquakes, typhoons or wars had managed to destroy him. With his quiet expression and folded hands, he symbolized peace and serenity, something many modern Japanese seemed to be lacking.

Afterwards the Fudge drove us to his parents' house by the sea. His wife and grown sons were also there and everyone received us kindly. The house had a beautiful garden and a terrace with a lovely view over the ocean. Since it was hot, we all walked down to the beach for a swim. A huge wave knocked me over immediately and tore the glasses from the Fudge's nose. But the water was beautifully refreshing and by the time we got back to the house a lovely meal had been prepared for us. We first had some sushi, novel and delicious to us back then, even though it is now commonplace in North America. Afterwards tempura was served. The deep-fried fish and vegetables tasted great. Very happy with our day, we drove back to the city.

On our last evening in Tokyo we had dinner with the Protestant missionaries in whose guest house we were staying. We gave them our bicycles and they prayed for us.

SEPTEMBER 1957

We were so happy to finally leave the big city of Tokyo. We rode on brand new scooters and were accompanied by two men from Fuji Industries and a car full of reporters. The day was spent taking pictures and finally putting up camp next to a little lake up in the mountains. The air was almost cool there and so refreshing compared to the heat in the valley. The next morning the two men from Fuji Industries wanted to take the new scooters home and leave us with the old ones. This would have been fine, except one of them wouldn't start and it took a mechanic two hours to get it fixed. We finally told them either to give us the new scooters or we would do without. This ultimatum caused great consternation and several telephone calls to Tokyo. But in the end we got the new scooters and, after many farewells and good wishes, we were on our own.

The southern part of Japan is quite different from the north. Everywhere there were palm, fig, mandarin and banana trees. It was also hotter and much more humid. The rice, which had just been planted when we arrived in Japan, was now in full bloom and would soon be yellow and ripe. We saw lots of tea plantations where Japanese green tea was harvested. We loved the bamboo forests; the trees appeared quite delicate and bent softly in the wind like young birches. Young bamboo sprouts are a delicious vegetable.

We first drove along the coast, which – like so many places in Japan – was breathtakingly beautiful. In some places there were huge walls to protect the road from the waves, but every so often a wave came right across and we got a free shower. We drove through Nagoya and from there along the beautiful Lake Biwa to Kyoto. This city was once the capital of Japan and has many lovely buildings and art treasures. We first visited the two big temples in the centre of town, both huge wooden buildings beautifully and richly carved. One of the temples is called Nishi Honganji (West) and the other Higashi Honganji (East). The supports and beams of these buildings consisted of huge, beautifully carved tree trunks, often with carved animal heads at the ends. I especially liked the curved lines of the roofs and colourful tiles. Every temple had at least one room with a big Buddha surrounded by his followers or saints.

The Shinto shrines were quite different from the Buddhist temples. Their symbol is the Torii, the red entrance gate. There are many different gods within the Shinto religion. One who is much revered, liked and also feared is the fox, a sly and cunning god. People who wanted special wishes granted bought certain pieces of paper and hung them up on trees or next to their favourite deity. Many of the gods wore a hat or a kind of bib, which were donated by people suffering from head or neck troubles hoping to be relieved of their pain. We often noticed small heaps of stones next to a deity. They were put there by believers who promised so many pilgrimages to this specific shrine. The stones helped them to keep count.

In the evening we once more walked to those old and holy places that were an oasis of peace in the centre of town. All the stone lanterns were lit, the moon shone brightly and after the hot day the evening air was cool and pleasant. All this, together with the ancient trees, the noise of the crickets and the curved outlines of the roofs, appeared to us more Japanese than anything we had experienced before.

The next morning we visited the Heian Shrine, the most famous in Kyoto. The red-coloured buildings stood in almost mathematical order. We loved the garden with the small lakes, the bridges, the blooming trees and plants. Everything here seemed to be in exactly the right place, and was built and planted with love and care. We visited one shrine that was dedicated to a holy cow and whose surrounding garden was full of stone cattle. In the Kinkakuji temple gardens we admired a golden pavilion that shone brightly in the morning sun. After a visit to the imperial palace and Nijo castle we scootered on to Nara.

Nara, too, was at one time the capital of Japan. This city was smaller than Kyoto but also a jewel of art and architecture. In the biggest wooden building in the world, we stood in awe in front of a Buddha who had been sitting there for over 1,300 years surrounded by grim-looking guards with huge dreadful heads. We spent almost a whole day in this temple complex and the surrounding parks where tame deer roamed. We loved the richly decorated five-storey pagoda and a shrine decorated with hundreds of cast-iron lanterns, each one different. The trail leading up to this shrine was adorned with another

2,000 lanterns, this time made out of stone. We were told that on a special holiday once a year all these lanterns would be lit. The Nara temple complex is situated next to a mountain and surrounded by ancient, shady trees that help make it cool and peaceful.

We didn't spend much time in Osaka, a big, industrial coastal city, but drove on through quite heavy traffic to Kobe, where we visited the Ritter family. They had a lovely villa up on the mountain with a beautiful view over the city and Osaka Bay. We continued along the coast to the small town of Akashi, from where we took a ferry across to Awaji Island, which seemed to consist of only rocks and ocean. We were driving on the coastal road to the main town of Sumoto, when we discovered a dead person in the water. I wanted to swim out to it, but Sigrid thought we then would have to take the body out of the water and it would be better not to get involved. We later saw a hat floating along and wondered if it belonged to "our" body.

We experienced the worst storm on this island as a typhoon passed fairly close by. The wind was so strong that trees bent almost to the ground and the rain came down in buckets. Luckily, just as we were going to put up the tent, we met a priest (from the Alsace in France), who offered us hospitality during the worst of the storm that lasted two days. While he was nice, he acted quite strange. He opened all the doors and windows for us and assured us over and over again that only he and his housekeeper were living here. He was weird in other ways too, and if the weather hadn't been so bad, we would have moved on.

That afternoon we went for a walk to the village. It was then only raining lightly, but while we were there all the elements broke loose. We first found shelter under village roofs, but when it continued to pour we ran back to the house and arrived there soaking wet. We found water in every room and wondered if the windows had been opened or if the rain came through the roof or walls. We weren't sure. When the typhoon was over, the sky first turned yellow, then red, then purple. Two minutes after the colour display, it was completely dark.

We left our host on a sunny morning, drove all the way south and took another ferry to the big island of Shikoku. Shikoku was almost untouched by foreigners and was an island of incredible beauty. We loved the coastal areas, the mountains and the lovely bamboo forests. We camped the night near Tokushima and drove the next day across the mountainous island in the narrow valley of the green Yoshino River. Many people recognized us from pictures in the newspapers and waved to us. It is fun to be alive, especially when the world is so beautiful!

When we reached Kochi, we went to the Rabbit Scooter Agency (as we always did in larger cities to get gas and maintenance), and we were received like VIPs. After the usual paper and radio interviews, there was a banquet for us at the best hotel in the town. First we had all sorts of delicious raw fish, such as crabs, shrimp, octopus, squid and lobster, which we dipped in soya sauce. Then we had tempura and, of course, rice. It was a delightful evening and, like many times before, we had to become actors in order to keep the conversation flowing. At times our Japanese hosts rolled on the floor, they laughed so hard. Of course, all the sake helped to make the evening a success. We really liked the Japanese, and we often had the feeling they liked us as well.

The next morning a young man from the scooter firm came to accompany us. We again followed the course of a river in a westerly direction further and further into the mountains. By evening we reached the highest point on the western side of the island and had a beautiful view of the green rice plains below us, as well as the inland sea with many islands beyond. While we were still in the mountains, our young man took us to a small museum where we had to see every exhibit. Then we followed him on narrow trails through a village and up and down the countryside. Then we left the scooters behind and walked to a gate that was opened before we had time to touch it. From there we walked on a narrow path through a jungle of plants to a stately house. We had no idea what was going on and became more and more curious.

We entered the house and the young man introduced us to its owner. We knelt down and bowed in greeting. A woman brought in *ocha*, green tea, and pears and grapes for our refreshment. Then the owner of the house appeared again, this time wearing a traditional Japanese warrior outfit. This consisted of extremely wide pants, a jacket and wide belt and a long sword in a sheath. Another man, also dressed as a warrior, came in. Both bowed first in front of the shrine, then in front of us and started to move in slow concentrated movements. The main actions consisted of quickly tearing the sword out of the sheath, jumping up, stomping with one foot on the ground and putting the sword back into the scabbard.

We spent the night near Matsuyama and the following morning took a ship across the Japanese inland sea. The boat wove its way among thousands of islands, some tiny and only covered with a few trees, others large with mountains and villages, and some in between. They were delightful to see and a pleasure to travel through.

Back on the main island of Honshu, we travelled the short distance to Hiroshima. We went to see the World Peace Church, which looked a bit like a bunker from the outside. The Japanese bishop himself, who spoke fluent German, gave us a tour of the church. (He did stress, though, that we should feel honoured that he himself did this for us.) Duly impressed, we learned that much of the interior of the church had been donated by German cities. The organ, for instance, came from Cologne, the baptismal font from Aachen, and the bells from Frankfurt. Hiroshima was quite a pretty town surrounded by mountains. Most of the Japanese houses had been destroyed by the atomic bomb, but what was left of the three or four stone houses that existed at that time still stood to remind people of that horrible day on August 6, 1945.

While we were still standing in front of the church, a busload of Americans arrived from a nearby base. One of them had read about us and told the others. The group invited us to join them for a tour of the town. Afterwards we went to a restaurant together, and before leaving we had to promise to visit them at their base.

Sigrid and I scootered a short distance south and then spent a wonderful evening on tiny Miyajima Island. We admired the red Torii that stood in the water, a shrine, a temple full of old paintings and pretty pagodas. The sun was just setting as we returned, adding an extra dimension to the already beautiful landscape. We couldn't find a place to camp along the coast, so we followed a trail into the mountains and found a creek. Since it was one of those perfectly clear and warm nights, we only unfolded our sleeping bags and slept under a tree. The concert put on by the crickets, the rustling noise of the wind in the trees and the sounds of water rushing down the mountain put us quickly to sleep.

It was a perfect Sunday morning when we woke up. The sun was shining and it was pleasantly warm. Sigrid had just taken a bath in the creek when a few farmers passed by. Sigrid tried to hide, but they had already seen her and were terribly amused by her embarrassment. We found the Japanese were a lot less fussy than Westerners about being seen in the nude. A few days earlier we had seen a stark naked man in conversation with another in the middle of the street. Men and women also bathed together, and most bathhouses had big windows anyone could look into.

Our life was very pleasant. The country was beautiful and the people delightful and kind. Since both of our watches had broken a long time ago, we got up when it was light, went to bed when it was dark and ate when we were hungry. Our scooters performed well, and we often wondered how we would have managed in the tremendous heat and humidity with our bicycles. Our food was relatively simple. In the morning we drank tea and ate bread with margarine. For lunch we usually had fruit and some bread, and at night we cooked rice and vegetables and ate some of Papa's canned meat, which lasted a long time.

Hugging the coastline, we were impressed over and over again by its beauty. We followed a narrow road up a mountain through rocks and cliffs and down again on the other side. Every once in a while we had a view of a bay whose shores were covered with pines. The roads were terribly narrow, seldom leaving room for two vehicles to pass. Sometimes not even a scooter and a car could pass; we had to get off and lean against a cliff in order to let a car or bus pass us by. The roads were practically all unpaved and in terrible condition. We seldom could go much faster than 20 kilometres an hour.

When we arrived at Iwakuni, the American base, we were already expected and everyone wanted to have us for a meal or an outing. As it had started to rain and didn't look as if it would ever stop, we were quite happy to be there and enjoyed all the attention we got. Actually, our stay became quite organized. One lady picked us up for breakfast, another for lunch, a third for tea, and so on. Then there were interviews for eight different newspapers and a radio station. Everyone was extremely kind, but the whole thing became too much for us. As soon as the first rays of sunshine appeared, we took our leave.

In Shimonoseki we took a ferry to the island of Kyushu, the last of the four main islands that make up Japan. Reporters were already waiting for us on both ferry terminals, but since they all knew the story of our lives already, we just had to pose for pictures and tell them how much we loved their specific part of the country. A lot of people also asked for our autograph, which seemed rather absurd. We drove along the east coast of Kyushu and all the way to the city of Beppu. There were a lot of hot springs in the area and in many places the water came boiling out of the ground, which is quite a noisy affair. We liked a lake that had hot steaming water. It had a high iron content and was bright red.

We left the coast in Beppu and drove inland toward the Mount Aso volcano. Many people had told us stories about this mountain, so we specifically packed our boots and were determined to climb it. We were very surprised when we found out that a brand new paved road led all the way to the top. It was an experience all the same, because we hadn't been on a blacktopped highway for a long time. The last stretch we climbed on foot, and then we looked into a huge crater. It is hard to describe the force with which the hot steam came out of the main crater and the hundreds of cracks all around. The noise sounded like thousands of steam engines working at the same time. Then there were the colours – yellow, brown, grey, white, red – and the smell of sulphur. Standing there, one could easily imagine the destructive forces of an exploding volcano.

In the evening we arrived in the city of Kumamoto. We saw some people on Rabbit scooters and wanted to ask them the way to the agency, but they disappeared as soon as they saw us. We were a bit surprised but managed to find the way on our own. At the agency everyone stood in front of the place and smiled at us expectantly. Only then did we see the huge banners draped across the garage: "Welcome Miss Sigrid Hirte – Welcome Miss Renate Hick." For once, we were speechless. The manager insisted on taking us to a hotel, and then we were shown the town. Later in the evening we had a great party with all our new friends from Kumamoto.

One of our friends escorted us to Arao, from where we wanted to cross the bay of Ariake. But we just missed the ferry by a few minutes. Yet nothing was lost. The director of the harbour invited us on a tour of the harbour and afterwards to a lovely meal, where the mayor joined us. When we were finally on the ship, the captain invited us to be his guests. He told us, "This ship is my present to you." (Since we didn't know how to run it, we decided to let him keep it.) Before we took off, many people threw us coloured paper ribbons and waved as the boat pulled away. The trip itself was beautiful. We were in first class, had fantastic food served to us and enjoyed the magnificent scenery all around. The captain himself escorted us to the right highway on the other side and said he hoped we would come back soon.

Shortly afterwards we were stopped by five people on scooters who were sent from Nagasaki to escort us there. Again, the countryside was very beautiful. The rice had turned a yellow-green colour, which looked like sunshine, and in between grew big red flowers. This contrasted with the dark-green hills, the deep-blue ocean, the green rivers and the light-blue sky. The people, too, wore more colourful kimonos than in other parts of the country. On our way we passed the town of Isahaya, which recently had been almost completely destroyed by floods. As beautiful as Kyushu was, the people there were never far away from natural disasters such as typhoons, earthquakes, floods, volcanic eruptions and mudslides, which seemed to occur far too often.

Nagasaki is known for being a Catholic town. More than 300 years ago, the Japanese persecuted all Christians and tried to exterminate them. That only made them all the stronger. Later, Catholics from other parts of the country came to Nagasaki and joined the Christian underground movement.

When we arrived we were taken to a hotel in Nagasaki that had been reserved for us. We again met many delightful people. The next morning we were given a tour of the city in the pouring rain and shown the Nagasaki Atomic Bomb Museum. A mountain divides Nagasaki into two parts – the bomb destroyed only half the city.

We had an extremely interesting trip to the Sakai Bridge, which connects two islands. Unfortunately, the roads were so muddy that we got stuck several times. Together we had to push the scooters out, and a few times our shoes remained in the morass and we had to go back to look for them. It was simply incredible. Once in a while one of our scooters slid into a ditch, or one of us was thrown off when the wheels bumped against a big rock hidden in the quagmire. We were covered in mud from head to toe when we finally came to a better road. In the first village we reached, people, upon seeing us, laughed so hard they almost rolled in the mud themselves. Then they got hoses and Sigrid and I – as well as our scooters – got hosed down. Afterwards we stopped at the next creek and washed our clothes and our hair. Luckily, the sun came out and in no time everything was dry. We proceeded to the city of Fukuoka.

In Fukuoka we were received like royalty. We were given two really nice policemen to escort us from place to place. The director of the scooter agency gave us a banquet and invited two German people who also helped to organize the next day's activities. First, we went to a puppet maker who formed his puppets out of clay and then painted them. Then we went to the main shrine, where the head priest awaited us. It was a holiday and many people were visiting to pay their respects. They clapped their hands (to make their presence known to the gods), prayed, clapped some more and threw money in the boxes. Many believers also brought small baskets full of ocean sand to have it blessed. This sand was then thrown over their heads for protection, especially before going on a journey.

A priest gave us some cypress boughs with small pieces of paper hanging from them that contained prayers he had blessed with great ceremony. We were directed to take the boughs, go to the altar, bow deeply in front of the goddess, who was the first empress of Japan, and drop the cypress boughs at her feet. Afterwards the head priest threw blessed sand over us to assure us of having a good journey and gave us a small basket of sand to take along just in case. Finally, a young priestess danced for us, accompanied by the music of a drum and a flute. She danced slowly with controlled movement and great beauty.

Next we had the opportunity to see a Japanese wedding. The bride and groom had just drunk their sake, which completed the wedding ceremony and made them husband and wife. The bride wore a traditional wedding dress, which consisted of layer upon layer of kimonos. Her hair had been lacquered into the traditional style and her face was made up heavily. She was a pretty but shy little bride.

In the evening a special banquet was arranged. When we were eating, a young girl came in to play the koto for us, which is a 1–2-metre-long instrument with 13 strings. The music of the koto, as well as that of the shamisen (a three-stringed instrument) is fairly monotonous. The instruments are used more often to accompany singing or other musical instruments. We had beef sukiyaki for dinner, which was cooked on the table. Everyone fished choice morsels out of the pot and dipped them in raw egg to cool them off for eating.

The next day we were escorted out of town by two of our hosts, and after a fond farewell we were on our own again. We drove the short distance to Kitakyushu and Moji and said *sayonara* to this beautiful island. Unfortunately, it started to rain and it looked as if it wouldn't stop for a long time. We now rode along the west coast of Honshu, which was quite thinly populated. In spite of its natural beauty, it was called the "Shade Side of Japan." Maybe the shady part referred to the weather. It just rained and rained. It got dark and we still hadn't found a place to camp. So we just kept going, always wondering when we would get stuck in the mud. Then we discovered what looked like an empty hut beside the road. We checked it out. It only had a few tools inside, but the roof leaked quite badly. Still, this was better than the rain outside. We put up the tent on the dirt floor, cooked some food and went to sleep.

Very early the next morning, when it was still dark, a construction crew woke us when they came to pick up their tools. They were extremely surprised to see us, but were very nice. They all knew us already from the newspapers. We quickly got dressed, had a nice chat with the men, packed up and continued riding through the rain. Around noon we found another empty house and a nearby spring. We stopped to make some hot tea and eat some food. We reached Hamada in the evening, where a father and his sons ran the scooter agency. They invited us to spend the night in their huge home, which housed uncles, aunts, grandparents, apprentices and whoever else had some business with the firm. We were introduced to everyone and each of them wanted to do something special for us. It was rather touching. After dinner we went out partying with the sons of the family.

Before we left the town, we went to see a fish auction. It was a lively place where the catch of the previous night was auctioned off. We were also invited to visit a fish cannery, which was quite interesting – and smelly. The sun came out and the drive along the west coast was incredibly beautiful, so beautiful, in fact, that it is still impossible for me to describe. Unfortunately, it became quite cold as we drove up a narrow road to a pass and from above looked way down to the ocean. Then we rode our way down between cliffs and other natural obstacles. In the evening we watched a sunset that was the most beautiful we had ever seen. There wasn't a colour that wasn't represented in the sky.

Shortly before the city of Matsue, we found a hidden campground and decided to spend the night there, not knowing that the radio had announced our arrival and the scooter agency had reserved a hotel and prepared a banquet. They even sent out an escort to meet us, but our tent must have been hidden from the road. The visit the following day still turned out well. We were shown the city and the old castle and everything else they thought we should see. We scootered on to Tottori in the afternoon and were invited by a Norwegian missionary family to spend the night. The lady of the house was extremely funny and we had a really good time.

We left the coast and drove into the mountains on very narrow roads. It was here my gear shift broke and it took almost all day to have it repaired. First Sigrid had to pull me into the next village, where parts had to be delivered from the next town. The following day was Sunday and it rained and rained. We found an empty hut and made breakfast there. Two Japanese, also on scooters, stopped to ask if we needed help. We said no and invited them for breakfast. They insisted on coming with us for the next 100 kilometres and we parted as good friends. We spent the night in Kyoto in the youth hostel.

The road to Nagoya was extremely bad and there was quite a bit of traffic, so we were happy to return to the less populated mountain areas. It was still raining a little, and when we saw a small temple hidden under some big trees, we decided to spend the night there. While Sigrid went down to the fast-moving creek to get water for cooking, I made the beds near the temple entrance while Buddha looked on. The stars came out later on, and we were happy to be here in this secluded spot under Buddha's protection.

We rode in a northerly direction toward Matsumoto, along a narrow river valley, and then south again past pretty Lake Suwa. People were harvesting grapes and invited us to share their bounty. Before we parted, they gave us a big bag of grapes to take along. We camped next to a river, but it was so cold that we couldn't get into our sleeping bags fast enough.

OCTOBER 1957

The next day, which was the first of October, I was riding peacefully along the road when suddenly a little boy on a bicycle, with his little sister on the back, shot out of a driveway right into my path. In order to avoid him, I crashed into a ditch and the two kids fell off their bikes and screamed as if I'd attempted to murder them. In no time people came running from all sides. After they'd found out nothing had happened to their little darlings, they helped to get my scooter out of the ditch and told me to drive more slowly. (How much slower than 20 kilometres per hour can one drive?)

We climbed quite a high pass and rode through the Sasago Tunnel. When we came out at the other end, we were rewarded with a most beautiful view. There was the snow-covered peak of Mount Fuji looking out of the clouds. This scene was so lovely and came so unexpectedly that we stood staring in amazement for the longest time. Then we rode down the mountain as close to Fujiyama as possible. It was very cold. While Sigrid looked for water, I collected some straw and wood and we made a little fire to warm us. I got quite sick afterwards and did not sleep well.

The night was cold and clear. The full moon was still in the sky when we got up to climb Mount Fuji. We hiked for a few hours through a pretty fall forest, and when it got light we marched on through areas covered with lava to finally reach the snow line. I didn't feel well at all and had to force myself to go on. The whole climb became a big blur. I only know that we were back at our camp 14 hours later, tired, cold and dirty. We decided not to camp but instead to go to a small hotel where we soaked in a hot tub for at least two hours to get some warmth back into our bodies.

We reached Tokyo at noon and now Sigrid didn't feel well. She went to bed while I made calls that had to be made and saw people who had to be seen. A parcel from Papa and Mama awaited us with lots of good things in it: cookies, salami, ham and blouses tailored for us. We were again overwhelmed by their kindness. In the evening we met up with Fanny, who was back at university, and had dinner together.

The last few days in Tokyo were very busy. When we wanted to return the scooters to Fuji Industries, the company said we could keep them and even paid for the freight to Calcutta, along with acquiring the necessary documentation for the vehicles. Mr. Matzuo, whom we had known only as a businessman, suddenly changed into a kind father figure looking out for the welfare of his daughters. It was quite amazing.

We spent a day in the factory, where we got extra parts to take along and where we were shown how a scooter looked from the inside and how to do simple repairs. In the evening we were picked up by Mr.

Matzuo himself, went to a sushi party and then to a judo game. Afterwards we watched some fencing and were impressed by the fast movements these athletes made. The party that followed was lots of fun. Everyone was a little tipsy and sang, clapped and danced. Yet another evening that passed too quickly. We found it hard to say goodbye to all our friends in Japan. We loved the people and the beauty of the country and hoped to come back one day.

On October 8, our dear Mr. Matzuo himself took us to the train station and put us on the train to Kobe, from where our ship would sail. He gave us some last-minute fatherly instructions and then we were off.

In Kobe we had to arrange for permission to export the scooters. Luckily, Mr. Matzuo had most of the papers already prepared and the whole thing was much less of a hassle than we thought it would be. We had bought tickets on a freighter from Kobe to Calcutta for US$130 each, which was very reasonable. The ship left at midnight.

Sayonara Japan.

CHAPTER 5

INDIA AND NEPAL, 1957–58

OCTOBER 1957

We spent a little over three weeks on the ship, the *Sangola*, which took us from Kobe, Japan, to Calcutta (now Kolkata), India. It turned out to be a most enjoyable sea voyage. We made friends with everyone; the passengers, the deckhands, the engineers, the officers and the captain all tried to make our journey as pleasant as possible.

There were quite a variety of people on board, including passengers from Britain, the United States, Japan, India, China, Thailand, Burma (now Myanmar) and Malaysia. The deck on which Sigrid and I had a large four-bed cabin was almost completely empty until two-thirds of the voyage was over. In Hong Kong some Chinese passengers boarded the ship, but the real crunch came in Singapore, where several hundred people crowded onto our deck.

The Indian women wore colourful saris, the Burmese, men and

women alike, wore rather dull material slung skirt-like around their hips. The men wore shirts, the women see-through blouses. All wore lots of jewels. There were also quite a number of turbaned Sikhs on the ship, as well as some Gurkha soldiers from Nepal and northern India. The Gurkhas are known for their bravery in combat. They were short and stocky, smiled readily and always wore a sword. The Chinese ladies wore long, tight-fitting dresses with stand-up collars and slits in their skirts all the way up to their hips. Some wore pyjama-like outfits that looked cool and practical.

From Kobe the ship travelled along the southern part of Japan and across the East China Sea to Hong Kong. it was wonderful coming from the quiet ocean into the busy Hong Kong harbour, where numerous steamers, freighters and other big ships from around the world were anchored. There were also many fishing vessels, sailboats, ferries and Chinese sampans with beak-like bows. It was one of the busiest and most colourful places we had ever seen. The city of Hong Kong is built on and around a mountain, has many modern buildings and from our ship looked absolutely magnificent.

Once inside the city we were somewhat appalled by the crowds in the narrow streets, the smells, the noise and the dirt. We were also appalled to see so many beggars and so much poverty. On the other hand, we were delighted with the colourful scenes around us; there was so much brightness and liveliness.

Alone or with other passengers or officers, we explored the city on foot and by bus. We were amazed at the many stores full of very reasonably priced consumer goods. Sigrid had a silk dress made by one of the numerous tailors, which was ready for pickup in a few hours. We took a tour to the top of a mountain and had a tremendous view from the mainland to the island of Hong Kong at night. Thousands of lights illuminated the shore and the mountain and only higher up the lights slowly thinned out. In the harbour we saw the quick-moving lights of the ferries, the bright lights of the ocean giants and the tiny lights of the slow-moving boats.

We stayed in Hong Kong for three days. Just before our ship left the harbour, we found, to our surprise, that a Chinese lady had arrived to share the room with us. She had an enormous amount of luggage but as it turned out never slept with us. She came in the morning, brushed her teeth, blew her nose, spit into the basin and disappeared again.

The food on the ship was most unappetizing. For breakfast we had potatoes with curry, for lunch, curry with rice, and for dinner rice with curry. Occasionally, some bones of an old goat or a tiny piece of meat broke the monotony. Luckily, we were always invited out while on land, which provided a nice change to our rather dull menu. Chinese food in a good restaurant is absolutely delicious.

From Hong Kong our ship went straight south through the South China Sea all the way to Singapore. It seemed to get hotter and hotter every day. I spent quite a bit of time on the bow of the ship because it was cool there and quiet. One day I saw a whole pod of dolphins and another time a fish that looked a bit like a dragon. But mostly I enjoyed the flying fish. Their fins were spread like wings as they skimmed 20–40 metres above the water. They were no bigger than bats and looked like glittering blue butterflies.

It was exceedingly hot in Singapore. The city itself was pleasant and very green. There were lots of tropical trees and blooming bushes, and everything was clean. We spent a few pleasant days and evenings in the city and surrounding areas. We would have liked to take our scooters down and drive them north to Penang, where we would have met the ship again, but we didn't get the necessary permit.

Then on we went to Penang, which is a little island just off the west coast of Malaysia. The state capital, George Town, was quite small and seemed to lack a proper centre. But it had any amount of temples, which were even more colourful and more decorative than the Japanese ones. While we were there it was a holiday, and we watched people buy some paper, pray over it, move it around their heads, spit on it, stamp on it and then burn it. All this burning made the heat even more unbearable. The temples were very crowded. The only quiet place belonged to a god sitting peacefully on a throne.

We also visited a snake temple. In the dim light it looked at first like any other temple. But then we saw the snakes – real ones, not carved! There were thousands of them in all shapes and colours, lying quietly on thrones and altars, around pillars and supports and wherever one looked. It was quite an experience. Later we stood in the marketplace and watched a man perform with snakes to the accompaniment of drums and flutes.

That evening a friend and I had dinner in town. When a rickshaw brought us back to the harbour, the last motorboat was gone and we had to hire a Chinese man and his boat to row us back to the ship. It was beautiful to see all the lights of the different vessels in the harbour.

From Penang our course was straight north along the Malaysian peninsula to Rangoon (now Yangon). As we approached the city, we entered the delta of the mighty Irrawaddy River. I watched from the bow as the fast-flowing waters of the river met those of the ocean, causing lots of eddies and strong whirlpools. It was quite early and the sun rose like a red ball promising another hot day. As we came closer we saw the shining metal roofs of the pagodas, one of which was supposed to have been real gold.

At the time of our visit, Rangoon appeared to be the worst capital city we had ever seen. It was small, dirty and squalid. Everything seemed to be falling to pieces. There were lots of beggars, many poor people and the most rotten smells. At one time Rangoon was supposed to have been a lovely city, but first the occupation by the Japanese, then an ongoing civil war and finally a policy of isolation had caused a steady decline. Much of the life of the city took place in the street. People cooked there, ate there and many also slept there. In the markets the meat hung on big hooks and was covered with flies; so was the fish. There were bugs all over the place, including great big beetles. Big and small temples surrounded the pagodas. In order to enter, we had to remove our shoes. Unfortunately, the floors weren't immaculately clean like in Japan but were instead covered with dirt, spit and excrement.

We had hoped to be able to travel overland to India, but we were told that fighting was going on all over Burma. We weren't allowed to leave the city, let alone travel through the country.

One evening we went out with some of the many acquaintances we had met on board the ship. At midnight, when it got a little cooler, we stopped at a restaurant for chicken and curry. People here didn't eat with chopsticks but used their fingers. At the end of the meal finger bowls were passed around.

Everyone on the ship was very kind to us. One of the engineers installed an electric fan in our cabin, which made the heat much more bearable. The chief engineer, who was on sick leave, invited us for tea every day and we usually kept him company for about an hour. The first officer also got sick and died shortly afterwards. He was buried at sea a few hours later and we said a prayer for him. It's amazing how fast this can happen.

On the last day in Burma some of the officers took us to a small lake where they had organized a sailboat. Unfortunately, there was no wind at all and we had to jump into the water and push the boat to get it across the lake. Swimming wasn't much fun because the water was too warm and brown – not a bit refreshing. However, we all enjoyed the outing.

When we got back to the ship we were quite amazed to find that two fat middle-aged Burmese ladies had moved into our room. (The Chinese lady had left us in Singapore.) These ladies sat all day cross-legged on their beds, smoking evil-smelling, green cigarettes. They even ate in the room. Quite expertly they rolled the food into little balls, which they then threw into their mouths. We didn't like all the smells of fish and rancid oil and curry and smoke in our bedroom, but we had to put up with it. Most of the time we weren't in the room anyway. The trip was coming to an end, much to our regret, as we had such a good time on board with all the wonderful people we'd met.

NOVEMBER 1957

It was quite exciting to arrive at the harbour in Calcutta, busy with sea and land traffic, and super busy with people. Calcutta seemed like an anthill, except instead of ants there were people everywhere. We went first to the YWCA and got a room with a high ceiling that had a huge fan rotating from its centre. Our next job was to secure our scooters from the harbour customs office. We were told this would take four or five days. However, we met a really friendly customs officer who knew other amicable people who took us to the harbour customs boss. By the end of the day we had our scooters. The boss even had gas brought to the shed where the scooters were stored. By evening we happily drove off.

We found out gas was quite expensive in India; we wondered whether or not we could afford it. We were even thinking of sending the scooters home on a boat. But luckily we met an oilman who invited us to a party attended by influential people working for Mobil Oil, Caltex and Burma Shell. After some discussion, Caltex offered to provide us with 50 gallons of gas in return for some advertising. They also gave a wonderful party for us.

We kept meeting new people all the time and received one invitation after another, sometimes several in a day. I think white people here were quite bored and any new face helped to make life a little more interesting. We spent a day at an English club in a park-like setting, with an immaculately clean swimming pool. An Englishman who worked for a tea concern took us there. One evening we joined a calypso carnival in the city, another we had a get-together with all of our Asian friends from the ship. We went to an obscure Chinese restaurant where the food was so outstanding that I still remember it today, over 60 years later.

We spent ten delightful days in Calcutta but were glad when the time came to leave. The poverty in the city was so very depressing; there was so much of it. One of our new English friends who owned a cookie factory asked us if we wanted to take some cookies along. We said yes, and he arrived with a carload of them, all packed in square metal containers. We loaded a few boxes onto our scooters, but there was no way we could take them all, so we handed the rest to poor-looking people, of which there was a steady supply. They all were quite surprised, took the boxes and walked away quickly. Dave, our tea friend, came at the last minute and brought us each a bottle of wine. We had to carry it in a bag around our shoulders; there was absolutely no more room in the pack.

We drove north toward Nepal through a flat, dusty, dried-out land, filled with people who appeared to be very poor. We heard that the monsoon had dropped very little rain on the Bay of Bengal region, which resulted in the worst rice harvest in 50 years. After two days we reached a lake. The water looked fairly clean and we put up our tent and swam in the water. The next day we reached the city of Patna and the river Ganges. Since there was no bridge to cross it, we had to wait a couple of days until we found a ship that brought us across the wide river. On the other side were miles of sand; we couldn't ride our scooters without getting stuck. We actually had to push them, which turned out to be quite a job in the heat and dust. After a few kilometres of such "slave labour," we came to a train station and happily boarded the scooters and ourselves for the relatively short journey to Muzaffarpur. On the train we met some Indian freedom fighters who talked enthusiastically about their "just" cause, which was to reunite Pakistan with India, under Indian control, of course.

We spent a pleasant day in Muzaffarpur with a Russian gentleman who stopped us in the street, invited us to his house and told us over and over again how much he enjoyed our company. It was always difficult for us to leave the next day, as people couldn't understand why we didn't want to spend more time with them.

We continued to drive north, but about 50 kilometres before the Nepalese border the road suddenly ended and we found ourselves on a trail covered with about 15 centimetres of pure dust – what a pleasure in the heat! After struggling for several hours we reached a river and wondered how we would cross it. However, that proved to be no problem, as some men came along with a raft and, with much laughter and noise, took us across. Not long afterwards we came to the next river. This one had a bridge, except it had just caved in under a heavy vehicle. It took a lot of combined effort to take first one scooter then the other across. Then we came across yet a third river. We found lots of bricks and built our own bridge through the deeper section of it. Finally, dirty, dusty and sweaty, we reached the town of Raxaul on the Nepalese border, where we saw our first Nepalese riding on an elephant.

The Indian customs officers told us that the road ended here but that we could travel another 50 kilometres inland by train. We left our scooters with the border guards and took the train the next day. It was a funny steam train: tiny, ancient and slow, but it did take us into the Terai, a damp hot jungle area of Nepal. Tigers were still supposed to roam there and malaria was widespread. An equally ancient, slow and dilapidated bus took us another 30 kilometres out of the jungle and into the foothills. Here we loaded our packs onto our backs and walked like the rest of the people in this country.

It was very hot and our packs were heavy as we constantly climbed uphill. When we finally reached a pass, we had a wonderful view of glaciers and snow-capped mountains. Someone pointed out Mount Everest and several other famous peaks. We were very impressed. After a short rest, we continued way down into the valley and up again over the next pass until we were completely exhausted and put up our tent for the night. All the farmers and herders from the area watched as we performed our tent chores and ate our simple meal. While we lay in the tent we listened to a shepherd playing his flute.

The next day we had to cross another pass, but then we saw Kathmandu, the capital of Nepal, way down in a wide valley. Nepal was completely different from anything we had seen so far. The people were incredibly dirty but always happy and ready to stop and laugh. We were told that the government liked to make things difficult for foreigners and that it was almost impossible to get a permit to travel out of the Kathmandu Valley.

Most of the people in this country were farmers and shepherds. Many earned some extra money as porters and carried enormous loads from one place to another. Except for the Kathmandu Valley, there were no roads. One was being built through from India and was supposed to be ready in another year or two. We were told there was quite a bit of trade between Nepal and India and also Nepal and Tibet. A journey to Lhasa in Tibet would take approximately 35 days. The Tibetans exchanged sheep, goat wool and salt for barley and rice.

Many Nepalese men had several wives and married quite young. But only the rich could do that. The poor could often only afford one woman per family, whom two or even three brothers would share. The king, who had died two years earlier as a relatively young man, was married when he was 7 years old to two sisters, aged 4 and 5. He had his first son when he was 14. His second son, who was born a month later, was the present king.

When we entered the Kathmandu Valley we thought we'd entered a magic land. Everything was so different and strange. Everywhere we looked stood exotic temples and pagodas, statues of strange gods, elaborate palaces, busy bazaars and houses without windows but intricately carved shutters. There was only one car in Kathmandu, belonging to the king, which had been carried in pieces across the mountains from India.

Kathmandu had only one hotel, belonging to a Russian by the name of Boris. He kindly gave us permission to camp in the hotel garden. He also introduced us to quite a few people, among them a Swiss man by the name of Schulthess. Mr. Schulthess told us that a young Swiss cheese maker, by the name of Sepp Dubach, was living in the small village of Langtang, right next to the Tibetan border, teaching the Nepalese how to make cheese. He also told us that, if we wanted to, we could travel there with one of his porters who was set to leave the next day with supplies. He suggested we sneak into the mountains since we wouldn't get a permit, and that we buy supplies to last us and our guide at least ten days. We were very excited by the prospect of entering the Nepalese mountain world and ran off to the bazaar and bought 20 pounds of rice, five pounds of dal (lentils), five pounds of sugar and one pound each of salt and tea. We were ready for a two-week trip.

The next morning a Tibetan came to pick us up. He carried part of the food and we carried the rest, plus our tent and sleeping bags and a few warm clothes. Our Tibetan, whom we called Knuelle, was amazingly dirty (you could also smell him miles away). I don't think his hair had ever seen a brush or his face a washcloth. His face actually had a crust of dirt on it and whenever he sweated (which was quite often) little rivers ran down his face between dirt banks.

We marched all day through hill country and arrived at a pass in the evening. Knuelle made a fire and cooked rice and dal, which we ate with great appetite, as we were terribly hungry. When we were finished we watched Knuelle, who continued eating until the last lentil and grain of rice was gone. The snow peaks looked great in the evening light but were even more beautiful in the morning when the first rays of sunshine hit them. The snow line began at approximately 4500 metres.

We began to live like the Nepalese and, like them, had only two meals a day: one at around 10 a.m., and the other before the sun went down. Knuelle had a limited English vocabulary, which consisted of "ja, ja, yes, yes," and "finish." Every morning before the sun came up, we heard his "yes, yes" call, which meant we had to get out of our warm tent into the cold. We got warm as soon as we started hiking, and once the sun came out it quickly became quite hot. Hiking for several hours without any food in our stomachs made us terribly hungry, and we could hardly wait for Knuelle to make a fire and start cooking.

These seven days in the mountains of Nepal were wonderful. We hiked up one mountain range after another and down again on the other side along fast creeks and waterfalls. We got higher and higher and closer and closer to the snowy peaks. We passed through several villages, such as Trishuli, Betrabi and Dhunche, and were appalled at how poor the people were. Yet they always laughed and waved. The houses were quite well built, usually with brick and wood, only instead of glass in the windows they had carved shutters that kept some of the cold out but made the inside very dark. The fields were built in terraces quite high up the mountains. The tools used were very primitive. People were thrashing wheat or barley with sticks, grinding grain in primitive watermills and spinning wool with little hand spindles. Everywhere people asked us for medicine, and in some cases showed us their wounds or hurting body parts. We only had a few aspirins with us, which we handed out. We felt very bad that we couldn't do more.

Most evenings after dinner Knuelle disappeared into the next village or hamlet to drink *chang*, the local barley beer, and to spend the night in one of the houses there. But one evening he indicated he wanted to sleep with us in the tent because there was danger about. He truly appeared scared, but there was no way we could let this evil-smelling, lice- and flea-ridden man sleep next to us. We told him he just had to stay outside, so he curled up right next to the flap of the tent and we all made it through the night.

After seven days of travelling, we reached the beautiful Langtang Valley, our destination. High mountains such as the Langtang Lirung (7234 metres), the Loenpo Gang (6979 metres) and the Xixabangma (8012 metres), which frame the valley, form the border between Nepal and Tibet. The people living there were all Tibetans. A river, fast and cold, travelled through the valley, and the jungle-like forest was full of monkeys, wild pigs and even leopards. In the evening we reached the place where the young Swiss fellow, Sepp Dubach, lived. He had already been there for seven months and was quite surprised to see us.

The first thing he said was, "Where are your porters?" Like all white people here, he thought we weren't able to carry our own belongings.

We had looked forward to sleeping in a real house again, especially since it got quite cold at night. We also looked forward to sitting at a table. But Sepp lived in an old barn that was only partly roofed. He and his Tibetan workers sat on logs around a fire on which they cooked, into which they spit and around which they ate and slept.

For the night we were assigned a spot in the barn on some soft hay and were quite cozy. The next day Sigrid didn't feel so well and decided to rest all day. Sepp went hunting, one of his favourite pastimes, while I walked up the river and washed from head to toe. I returned around noon, wonderfully refreshed and very clean. One of the Sherpas had boiled some potatoes and eggs and shared them with us. We really enjoyed this treat. Sepp returned with four mountain goats that the men started to clean, cut up and cook.

Sigrid felt better, so we spent the afternoon exploring the valley. In the evening we had yoghurt, which we tried for the first time mixed with tsampa, roasted barley flour. It tasted quite pleasant, except the yoghurt containers were so filthy that it took our appetite away.

Sepp asked us if we wanted to go hunting with him the next morning, and I thought it would be a great idea. Sigrid was still not up to it. Sepp woke me up before sunrise. Outside, everything was white with frost and there was ice on the water. We climbed steadily from the valley floor, which must have been about 3000 metres to over 4000 right to the tongue of a glacier. We roamed for several hours but didn't see any animals.

Just as we were ready to give up, we saw a wild pig below us. While

I waited, Sepp quietly climbed down. Unfortunately, the pig saw or smelled Sepp and moved on. Sepp followed and this game went on. Then I heard a shot and followed the sound. I found Sepp, but we couldn't find the pig. Finally, he asked me to run down and send up his men. It took me an hour to get down, sliding over loose rock and getting caught on lots of underbrush. At one point I landed in the middle of a troop of monkeys, every one of which was almost as big as I was. I think I scared them – they certainly scared me.

I continued to run downhill until I reached our barn, where everyone looked surprised when I arrived alone and out of breath. Now I had to somehow explain that Sepp needed help to find and transport the pig. I went down on all fours and made the sounds of a wild pig, mimicking Sepp with his gun and pointing to the mountain. Sigrid killed herself laughing, but the men were merely puzzled. I continued to dramatize the story. Eventually, one guy caught on, told the others and pretty soon they were all laughing and travelling up the mountain. The wild pig arrived at the camp just before sundown. The men made a big fire and burned off the pig's hair. Then all the people from the village came and cut big chunks out of the pig, which were then roasted on many little fires. Sepp, Sigrid and I also got some delicious and juicy pieces of meat. Later on the Tibetans danced and sang and drank great quantities of chang. We tried it too and joined in the merrymaking.

The next morning we hiked with Sepp for a few hours up the valley to a hut where the cheese was manufactured. The cheeses, as big and round as wagon wheels, were washed, wrapped and tied to pack boards the porters transported to Kathmandu. We sampled some of the cheese and found it quite delicious. It tasted a bit like Emmenthal or any hard cheese. It was made from yak's milk. Living high up in the mountains, yak cows produce about half a litre of milk per day, but this milk has a high fat content of about 13 percent.

On the way back we stopped in the village and visited Knuelle at his house. He was very pleased we had come to visit him and told his family all sorts of stories about us. Of course, we didn't understand a word but joined in the general laughter. After we had some chang, we took our leave. We stopped to say hello to the lama and then went back to our barn, where Sepp was packing his few belongings and organizing the loads for the porters to carry to Kathmandu the next day. We were lucky to be able to return with the men and the summer's cheese harvest.

We left early for the trip back. There was Sepp, the two of us, two Sherpas and ten porters. One of the porters we called Curly because he had a head full of curls. Like Knuelle, whenever he sweated, whole rivers of dirt ran down his cheeks. We had lots of fun on the trip. Everyone was in high spirits and looking forward to the city.

One night we slept in an empty house and I woke up when a rat jumped over my sleeping bag. I chased it away. Sigrid woke up when someone tried to get into her pack. She slapped the thief's hand away and put the pack under her head for the rest of the night. Every day we moved further away from the mountains, the whole time regretting having been there for only such a short time. Yet, as everyone had told us, we were lucky to have been there at all.

Upon our return to Kathmandu, we found we'd become almost famous among the white people there; it wasn't every day that two girls went alone into the mountains without a permit. We were showered with invitations and enjoyed every one of them. We were quite pleased to meet Peter Aufschnaiter, one of the heros depicted in the film *Seven Years in Tibet*, during a visit to the Swiss Compound.

Again we camped in the garden of Boris's hotel and every morning we were awakened by a uniformed waiter who handed us our morning tea on a silver tray. When this happened the first time we were very astonished, but after a while we got used to it. Upon leaving we asked Boris if the waiter could come with us.

We visited many temples while in Kathmandu. People say there are more temples there than houses. One of them was the Naxal Bhagwati temple on the banks of the Bagmati River, a tributary of the Ganges, where the bodies of the dead were burned every morning and the ashes thrown into the river. Another was the Swayambhunath, a Buddhist temple up on a hill several kilometres away.

We really liked some of the houses in town. They all had the most beautiful carved windows, doors and supports, all of dark brown, almost black, wood. We also spent a day walking to Patan, where we admired the erotic stone carvings on the temples. One day we hiked to the village of Boudhanath to see the temple that had big eyes painted on all four sides of the central tower. These all-seeing eyes of the Compassionate One looked out over the valley to the four points of the compass. As a special honour, we were invited to visit the Shini Lama, the Tibetan abbot of the monastery. He was very friendly and showed us the temple, as well as lovely old *tankas*, paintings on cloth, which is an ancient Buddhist art form. We then had Tibetan tea with him. This was a concoction of tea, rancid butter, salt and soda. It's supposed to be quite nourishing. The Tibetans drink vast quantities of this tea.

Some friends of Boris lent us bicycles and we enjoyed travelling the roads and trails around Kathmandu. We didn't have to watch out for traffic, as there were no cars or trucks. We met up with some young Frenchmen, and when we saw a huge crowd next to the government buildings we all went to investigate. The king had just dismissed several members of the ruling body and people were demonstrating. One of the French fellows jumped on top of his bike and yelled, "*Vive le roi de Nepal!*" Every time he did this the crowd yelled with enthusiasm. It was really quite funny. But Sigrid and I thought they got a bit carried away, so we decided to leave. To our astonishment the crowd followed us. This was more attention than we wanted; we jumped on our bikes and speedily pedalled off.

We had such a good time in Nepal and had met so many nice people that we hated to leave this hospitable place. Never before had we loved a country and the people in it as much as this one, nor had we ever seen a place as different as Nepal. A Swiss fellow offered us a ride in his Unimog, a kind of Jeep, across the partly constructed road to India. We accepted. Even though we only averaged ten kilometres per hour, it was better than walking. From a 3000-metre-high pass we had a last view of Kathmandu and the Himalayas. Then it was back into the lowlands and onward to new adventures.

DECEMBER 1957

At the border the Indian customs officers had given us up for lost or dead so were pleased to see us. We were persuaded to tell them about

160

our adventures while drinking endless cups of sweet tea. Then we got on our scooters and, waving goodbye, happily drove off into an unknown wide world.

We were once more in India among the dirt and dust, the poverty and the crowds full of so many wild-looking people. However, while all of this had astonished and bothered us in the beginning, it didn't anymore. Now we felt part of the scene.

We had travelled for about half a day when the road suddenly ended. A narrow path brought us to the Ganges, where a small boat took us to the other side. For several hours we drove on narrow and dusty trails, always leaving several kilometres between us because of the enormous dust clouds. The only living things we saw were monkeys. Just before it got dark, we reached a house occupied by an Indo-European. He was very happy to see us and invited us in for supper. He also insisted we stay the night. The only means of transportation this man had was an elephant, and all three of us went for a ride on it the next morning. Then he took us on a tour of a sugar factory he managed. Dozens of ox carts full of cane sugar were standing in line to be unloaded, both people and animals waiting patiently for their turn.

We finally reached the road to Gorakhpur and then the city. Here we were to look up a Dr. Saraf, whose address had been given to us by Sigrid's mother. He turned out not to be the most pleasant character, but he had a sweet little wife. He insisted on showing us off to all his friends. He also wanted to sleep with us, to "protect us" as he pointed out. We were glad when we finally got away.

When we left Gorakhpur, we were still the only motorists on the road. Once we got on the main Calcutta-Delhi highway, things changed only a little. There were elephants sharing the highway with us, camels loaded with goods and people, water buffalos mostly pulling carts of sugar cane and hundreds of monkeys sitting by the wayside. There were also huge vultures so intent on feeding on dead animals that we almost had to touch them with our scooters before they'd make room for us on the narrow, tree-lined road. What we enjoyed most were the many birds in all colours and sizes: wild ducks, pheasants, peacocks.

We always camped at night, but even in the most secluded spot people seemed to appear from nowhere and stand around watching us silently. In the mornings we usually got up before sunrise and travelled while the air was still cool. We really enjoyed sitting on our scooters, travelling through this strange land where there was always something new to see.

We travelled from Gorakhpur south to Benares (also know as Varanasi) and spent a day in this holy city. The place was horribly crowded, especially on the banks of the Ganges where people immersed themselves in order to purify not only their bodies but also their souls. The rich and the poor, beggars, yogis, holy men – all were performing ceremonies of all types. The banks of the river were lined with temples, beautiful old houses, palaces and mosques. Steps led from the river up into narrow streets, some so narrow there was room for only one person or animal.

We had just left Benares when the gear shift on my scooter broke. We had to take the whole machine apart, and only when we put it back together for the third time were we successful. This took the whole day. A few days later my brake cable broke and Sigrid lost her sighting glass (for the gas). Her gas filter and brake liners were also worn out. We managed as best we could, usually losing a lot of time during repairs because of our inexperience. It was almost impossible to get spare parts and improvisation became our only chance at success, at least in regard to scooters.

The north of India is quite flat and in many places very dry, almost like a desert. We always had sunshine and blue sky. The days were warm and often hot, but the nights were bitterly cold. One evening we were so tired and cold that we stopped in Cawnpore (now Kanpur) at a school run by German nuns and asked if we could put up our tent in their garden. They were delighted to see us and insisted we stay the night in one of their spare rooms. When we left the next morning they gave us homemade Christmas cookies for the road.

The next day Sigrid lost a part of the gasoline system on her scooter and all her gas ran out into the dust. A friendly guy in a Jeep pulled her to the next town and stopped in front of the town hall. The mayor and some of his councilmen came out and invited us for tea and later for a tour of the town. We were taken to the bazaar, where we had to try all sorts of sweets, then to an open-air theatre where we were introduced to several actors who promised to reserve seats for us for the next show. Since the performance didn't start until 11 p.m., we were taken back to the town hall for a lovely dinner of curry, chapatis and puris. The theatre turned out to be a light opera of which we understood little.

The area depended on the manufacturing of textiles. We had a chance to visit some home weavers. They used the finest silk threads to weave the most wonderful patterned cloth. We were told that for a patterned silk sari (requiring five metres of material) three men worked three to four weeks to produce it. And then such a sari was sold for 200 rupees (Can$120). One can imagine how little the weavers earned.

As we spent more time in India, we came to like the Indians better. We got used to their way of speaking and acting. We often talked to the merchants when we did our grocery shopping or the owners of gas stations when we'd fill up our scooters. We often were invited for tea, for a meal or even to spend the night. One day we were in a house when a group of male relatives arrived from another town to arrange the marriage of their son to the 14-year-old daughter of the house. While the parents and relatives talked about the dowry, the young people were allowed to talk to each other. Another time a father showed us pictures of three girls and told us the life story of each. We were to help him choose the right wife for his son. Both Sigrid and I chose the same girl and he said that was the girl his wife had also picked. We wondered, did she become the happy bride?

The Indian women looked very pretty in their saris. Most ladies were slim and the colourful saris brought out their figures to advantage. In different regions of India the sari is wrapped around the body in a slightly different fashion. Many men wore dhotis, which consisted of white cloth wrapped diaper-like around their lower middle. Men also had the strangest hairstyles that were usually connected with their religion or caste. Some wore long locks, others had their hair tied up in a ponytail, yet others were completely bald or had a bundle of hair in the middle of their heads. The Sikhs covered their hair with a turban. At the time how I wished I knew more about Indian culture and religions. But affordable books weren't available; we could only watch and listen and try to learn.

People ate a lot of rice and curry. Most Indians were vegetarians. The food was extremely spicy, sometimes to such a degree that we couldn't tell what we ate. The sweets, too, were very different here; they were soft and very sweet. We tried whatever we were offered and liked almost all of it because we were always hungry.

We arrived in New Delhi the day before Christmas and drove to Robin's house, a friend of Dave in Calcutta. He and Suki (who shared the house with him) had to go to a wedding in the Punjab on Christmas Day (the son of a maharajah was marrying a German girl), so we were invited to stay in their house while they were gone. On Christmas Eve we went to the German Consulate to have our passports renewed, did some shopping, washed and ironed whatever we owned and then picked up Robin and Suki from work. We helped them do their shopping, had dinner together and saw them off at the railway station. We almost forgot it was Christmas, but the fact that we were in a house instead of a tent and had books to read and tea served to us made it a festive occasion.

We spent Christmas and Boxing Day sightseeing in Delhi. The new city was splendid, with wide roads, beautiful parks and impressive government buildings. The old city had narrow roads, huge mosques and temples, big crowds, bazaars and holy cows that always managed to run in front of our scooters.

Having worked on our scooters, when Robin and Suki came back we were ready to take off toward the city of Agra. In the evening we stopped to put up our tent near a small village, but the people said it would be safer for us to sleep in the empty schoolhouse, which had neither doors nor windows and a dirt floor. While we sat on a mat cooking our rice, someone brought us a little milk and someone else chapatis and a third person an oil lamp. We were quite touched.

I woke up in the middle of the night and knew something was sitting beside me, but it was too dark to recognize what. I waited for a while to adjust my eyes to the darkness, then quickly reached out to touch whatever was there. I knew then it was a person. I yelled, "Get out of here!" The person ran off and I jumped out of my sleeping bag, stumbling in the dark after whoever had been there. When I got back from this unsuccessful chase, Sigrid asked if I'd caught him. I said no, but I wondered afterwards what I'd have done if I had.

The following day we reached Agra, an old Indian city full of beautiful palaces and forts. We first saw the Taj Mahal and were immensely impressed with this white marble memorial built close to 400 years ago by the Mughal Emperor Shah Jahan for his favourite wife Mumtaz Mahal. We loved the perfect proportions and the rich stonework of the building, plus the beautiful gardens with small artificial lakes. The white marble of the Taj Mahal contrasted beautifully with the bright blue sky and the dark green of the parkland. We were happy to have had the privilege to see one of the Wonders of the World and, since the early 1980s, a UNESCO World Heritage Site.

On our journey toward Bombay (now Mumbai) we entered the land of tigers, and people warned us not to camp. The whole area was dry and hot and there was little vegetation. It was also sparsely populated. Every so often we drove through some hilly areas with the ruins of huge fortresses on top. The few cities we came through were surrounded by huge walls, and inside were too many people and animals and too much dust. The dust in India was truly terrible. In the evening our eyes were always red and painful from too much light, heat and dust. It was just as well that it was winter; the days were short and we were forced to rest our eyes for 12 to 13 hours each night. The further south we drove the warmer it became. At least we didn't have to freeze anymore during the night.

Near the city of Indore, we turned off the main road and drove toward Ajanta to see the famous Buddhist cave monasteries there. They date from 200–100 BC, more decorated caves being added during the fifth and sixth centuries AD. They were so well hidden in a narrow gorge that they were "lost" for 1,000 years and only recently rediscovered practically intact. These caves (there are 30 of them) were cut into the bank of a ravine and used as a college monastery. They consisted of a pillar-supported veranda behind which were 22 sanctuaries. The stone pillars were beautifully carved and the sculptures and frescoes inside were absolutely magnificent. Most were quite erotic and obviously dedicated to a god or goddess of love.

We spent the whole day in and around the caves and camped in the evening nearby. It was the last day of the year. While we lay in our sleeping bags, we reflected on the past 365 days and on all the amazing things we'd seen and experienced in Canada, Japan, Nepal and India. Would there ever be a year quite like it again?

JANUARY 1958

The traffic increased considerably as we approached Bombay and became really heavy once we got there. We stayed in one of Suki's apartments and had two servants at our disposal. However, we spent most of our time in the Lambretta scooter factory. The mechanics working there were really helpful and aided us with repairs and new parts and power-cleaned the machines. Driving in all that dust had been hard on our scooters.

We spent two weeks in Bombay, a city we liked more and more. In the evening the bay was decorated with a chain of lights and a fresh sea breeze came from the ocean. During the day the row of houses next to the beach looked pretty and colourful and reminded us of Nice in France. There were palm trees everywhere, and the well-kept gardens were full of flowers and blooming bushes. In contrast the centre of the city was hot, dirty, dusty and crowded with people, carts, animals, cars and trucks. On the weekend we drove with Suki to his weekend retreat 50 kilometres out of town. It was a lovely place next to a sandy ocean beach. We liked it so much that we spent a whole week there. The little house was great. Everything was open; instead of windows there were mosquito nets. Around the house were a small green lawn and bushes with big red flowers. Next to the lawn were the white sandy beach and the ocean. Except for one servant, we were all alone there. When we weren't swimming we were lying in the shade reading. I guess we needed a holiday from travelling.

But this luxury couldn't go on forever. We had to get back to town to organize our trip home. We didn't believe our scooters would be able to make the trip overland through Pakistan, Afghanistan, Iran and Iraq. We were looking for a ship to take us across the Arabian Sea into the Persian Gulf or the Red Sea. We visited quite a few shipping companies but couldn't find suitable passage. Just when we had decided to travel overland after all, the captain of a German freighter, the *Rothen-fels*, was willing to transport us to the Suez Canal for only a hundred dollars each. Our scooters were to travel free. We were told to be ready at the beginning of February. Needless to say, we were delighted.

In order to see a little more of India, we parted from our lovely cottage by the sea and travelled south through a hot and parched land. There was little water anywhere – even the riverbeds were almost completely dry. We arrived in Hyderabad and were taken by this city, which seemed more Indian than all the other cities we had seen. We admired the great big white palaces, the numerous fountains and also a river and a small artificial lake. We spent all day walking through the city, always followed by huge crowds, and enjoyed this magnificent, colourful and lively place.

We liked the south of India. It was hot and dry, but wherever there was a drop of water the most profuse vegetation resulted. During and after the rainy season this must be paradise. The soil was red, which looked more interesting than the usual grey earth. There were also mountains with roads winding up on one side and down again on the other. But the main elements were the sun and the dust. We drove hour after hour. It was hot and our eyes burned and the dust enveloped us, but we still found the land interesting and beautiful.

We had a lot of trouble with our scooters. Every day something went wrong: the brake cable broke, then the ignition, screws loosened and the carburetor fell into the dust. It was just one thing after another. Luckily, we had by now enough experience that we could help ourselves, but it wasn't fun spending hours trying to repair the scooters, especially during the hottest part of the day with no shade anywhere.

We seemed to be always tired and dirty and without water to wash. At night, when we stopped near a village, we often got only enough water to drink. Both Sigrid and I enjoyed good health during the trip, even though we often drank unboiled water and shared food with the locals. Our skin became so brown that we often wondered if people would still recognize us at home.

The Indian people were all very nice to us, but I'm sure they must have thought us quite strange. Whenever we stopped we caused a crowd. One day we halted to get gas and so many people stopped to stare at us that three policemen were needed to disperse the throng (and not very successfully either).

On an extremely hot day, about 100 kilometres west of Hyderabad, in an area bare of any shady trees, we saw one of many old fortresses. Since we were tired of riding our scooters, we walked through the huge complex. After a while I happened to look through a hole in the wall and saw below a small lake and a wall that acted like a dam. On the other side of the wall was a little waterfall that dropped the water into a creek that disappeared into the landscape. We climbed down and splashed and swam in the water and felt immensely refreshed and clean.

On the same day we had another interesting experience. Sigrid's brake cable broke very close to a mission built and run by a Methodist couple. We were invited in and shown around. There were neat little houses, a church, a school and a farm. The school was a boarding school for the children of the area and each child had to pay a rupee (less than a dollar) a month. But the children had to help on the farm, where rice, vegetables and fruit were grown. There were also cows and chickens. Mr. Gardener, the missionary, also employed the parents of the children in a small soccer ball factory he had built. He gave farmers seeds and plants and helped them in many ways. We were very impressed with the place, the discipline of the children and the cleanliness everywhere. Before we left, Mr. Gardener asked us to give a talk to the children and we told them about our trip through their beautiful country.

Further south, just as the road ended, we again met some missionaries who invited us in and didn't want to let us go again. They were Mennonites and their ancestors had been German. In the evening we went to a prayer meeting with them. First we sat in a circle and sang. Then one after another kneeled down and prayed aloud. Since they all said more or less the same, it got rather boring.

Quite a few Muslims lived in the region. The women were covered from head to toe, and even covered their faces when they saw us. I think many people believed we were men because we wore pants. Quite a few Parsees of the Zoroastrian sect also lived in the area. They were descendants of the Persians who settled in India in the eighth century to escape persecution. They decorated the floors of the entrances to their houses or a section inside the house with painting created with colourful powders that looked impressive and charming. Most houses were quite primitive, with one room only and built of sod. On one side of the room was the fireplace (the women squatted on the floor to cook), while on the other side mats were spread out for sleeping. We often spent nights in such a hut because the people were very hospitable and didn't want us to put up the tent. But we never liked it very much because there were so many insects.

In Bangalore (now Bengaluru), an almost-European-looking city, we met a German couple who insisted on taking us to their home. We really liked our stay with them. The people were interesting, the climate was pleasant because we were in the mountains, and the city seemed a lot cleaner than others. We met a Belgian traveller riding a Vespa (an Italian scooter) who had heard about us, and we spent a pleasant evening with him and his Indian friend. We also met a man from Frankfurt who worked at the same firm as my father. He promised to call my parents and send greetings. That Sunday, January 26, it was Republic Day. There were parades, speeches, folk dancing and theatre to mark the anniversary of India's constitution coming into force in 1950.

We then moved on to Mysore (now Mysuru), admired the Maharaja's Palace, the huge statue of a holy cow on top of a mountain, the elegant Summer Palace and a temple covered with beautiful stone sculptures.

On extremely bad roads we drove on to Belur and Halebidu to see the famous temples there. It was worth the trip. In Halebidu the stone temple was decorated with horizontal bands of sculptures of elephants, tigers, horses, lotus flowers and people. The stonework was extremely intricate and amazingly beautiful. There were also many sculptures of the monkey god, the elephant god and many others. As we walked around in awe, a group of young girls arrived all dressed in colourful saris. They made such a graceful and happy group among the temple treasures that we couldn't keep our eyes off them.

The month of January was coming to an end and we started our journey back to Bombay. Even though the roads were terrible, we enjoyed the hilly landscape and the many trees with their big red blossoms. We were glad when we arrived back on the paved Bangalore-Poona (now Pune) highway. We were stopped there by a young woman who stood by the wayside and waved frantically. She told us she was an American missionary and lived nearby with another woman. She begged us to come with her to the station and we did. The two young ladies lived there all alone. One, Gladys, was a nurse, and looked after about 60 patients daily who arrived with all sorts of ailments. Mary Lou, a Canadian, entertained the patients by playing hymns on her harmonica and telling them bible stories. Both Gladys and Mary Lou were so happy to have somebody to talk to besides each other and their patients. They outdid themselves with kindness toward us and begged us to stay the night.

In Poona we visited the Indian friends we had met the first time we came through. They were happy to see us, took us to their cool home with enormously high ceilings and introduced us to all their relatives – there were many.

The next morning we drove on to Bombay and right away went to see the Hansa Shipping Co. We were told the *Rothenfels* wouldn't leave on February 10 as planned but the next day. The captain suggested we spend the night on board and invited us to a party. That didn't leave us much time, but we managed to get to the post office to pick up our mail, get a visa for Egypt, go through the necessary customs formalities and arrive at the ship completely exhausted but happy we had made it on time. The next morning our ship steamed out of the harbour.

Soon India was lost on the horizon.

CHAPTER 6

EGYPT, TURKEY, GREECE AND HOME, 1958

FEBRUARY 1958

It turns out we were the only passengers on the *Rothenfels*. We had a cabin right next to the captain. It had two built-in beds, a chesterfield, table, chairs and a closet. There were no restricted areas for us on the ship, and everyone from the captain to the deckhands did everything in their power to make the days for us as pleasant as possible. What a holiday from travelling!

All the officers on board the ship were Germans, the rest from Pakistan. The food was excellent. We had German bread, German sausages, fried potatoes, cheese, Rote Grütze and many other types of food we hadn't tasted for a long time. There was even cake with the afternoon coffee. For the past three months we'd lived mainly on rice and fish. What a pleasant change this was!

We were never bored on the ship. Besides reading and writing letters, we helped paint the name of the ship and its city, Bremen, on all the lifesavers and lifeboats and also did some typing. Every morning we read the *Hamburger Abendblatt*, with the news transmitted from Germany. It was good to know for a change what was going on in the rest of the world.

We spent a few days anchored in view of Karachi, Pakistan, before getting the permission to land. Since the engineers had too much free time, they helped us get our scooters in shape. They even built a few new parts, the old ones being lost or broken. Every day the captain and the officers tried to talk us into returning with them all the way to Germany and told us all sorts of horror stories about the Arabs. But we wanted to see a little more before going home and still planned to leave the ship and its wonderful people at the Suez Canal.

We had a lovely time in Karachi. One of the customs officers showed us the town and its surroundings. The city, at that time, was quite new. It became the capital only after the British had left India in 1947, and after the country was divided between Indians and Pakistanis, or Hindus and Muslims. We liked Karachi; it was only missing trees and parks. Around the city was nothing but sand, and the only means of travel was the camel. It was even used to pull wagons. The Muslim women were all covered from head to toe, while the Pakistani men we met were all fanatics. All of them hated Indians and all insisted that Kashmir, an Indian territory, should become part of Pakistan because most of the inhabitants were Muslim (a conflict that continues to this day).

We spent another day with the same customs officer by the ocean and enjoyed it tremendously. In one direction was the Arabian Sea, in the other nothing but desert. We also had a chance to ride a camel, which could run faster than we thought. When a camel lets the rider get off, it first goes down on its front knees and the rider flies forward. A second later the back legs go down and the rider flies backward. Before he has a chance to recover, the front legs go all the way down and there is danger of falling over the head of the camel. But by then it's time to get off and to thank Allah that the rider is still alive.

We left Karachi and enjoyed being on "our" ship. We felt as if we belonged there. Everyone was so sweet and tried to spoil us. The cook loved it when we came for a visit to the kitchen and always had a treat for us. One day a young officer said, "When you leave us, it will be so boring again on the ship." We suggested that they get some other girls, but he answered that they would never find a replacement for us. One evening we had a big carnival party. Ernesto, our carpenter, played the accordion and we all sang and danced. Then we organized a polonaise through the whole ship and played games. When the captain finally decided to call it quits, we all went into the little carpenter workshop and continued to party.

We also played a lot of Ping-Pong and every evening had a tournament. It was the only chance to get some exercise, and with all the fantastic food we had, we needed it. It continued to get very hot. Even at night, it hardly cooled down. We entered the Gulf of Aden and hoped to stop in Aden, but our ship didn't get the promised freight and chugged on. But we passed quite close to the city hidden behind a giant rock.

In the Red Sea the waves became quite strong. I walked on deck and enjoyed the fresh breeze. Then I went up to the bridge and helped the second officer with his lookout duties. The rest of the afternoon was spent removing rust and painting. It was nice to do some work once in a while.

The next day we landed in Djibouti, which at that time was part of French Somalia. Djibouti was a small city. Nothing grew there. The houses had flat roofs and were all white. The sky and the ocean were blue and the sand grey. Sigrid and I took our scooters down and made an excursion inland. It was very hot and the huge emptiness all around us almost made us feel lost. The population was Arabic and African. We spent the next day swimming, which was fun, but the many little fish and weeds near the shore spoiled the fun a little.

Our next stop was Aseb in Eritrea. But we only stopped for a short while for repairs. In the evening we reached Port Sudan in Sudan. At 10 p.m., after we had finished a medical control, we went with the officers to a sailors' home directly on the beach. We spent half the night swimming in the pool and playing games, and when we got back to the ship we continued partying.

The next day we took our scooters off the ship. Two officers who happened to have a day off accompanied us. We explored the city and its surroundings. Port Sudan was also a desert town and once we left the white houses with their flat roofs behind there was nothing but sand. We thought the Sudanese tall, good-looking people, only their hair seemed dreadful to us. We were told they rubbed cow dung into it. They seemed to constantly scratch themselves with a comb stuck into their hair.

We spent four days in Port Sudan, but we never got bored. Every day brought something new. We used the facilities at the sailors' home, rented a rowboat and tried to cope with the waves, and even went to an outdoor movie. It got very cold once the sun went down and we wished we'd brought sweaters.

On the last evening the captain gave a dinner for us. It was a wonderful meal; the cook had outdone himself. We partied most of the night. The next day we reached the Suez Canal. The captain and the officers still tried to talk us into coming home to Bremen with them, and we were tempted. But we wanted to see Egypt and part of the Middle East before going back to Germany. It was hard, though, to say goodbye to all our friends. At the last minute the cook handed us a big parcel full of canned food, and then we were standing on the bank of the Suez, waving to all our friends on the ship. To be honest, we felt like jumping into the water and swimming after them. We were suddenly so alone!

MARCH 1958

We quickly left the Suez behind and before we knew it we were surrounded by desert. It was extremely hot and the sun dreadfully bright. Soon our eyes hurt from the sand and the sun. Yet there was no escaping either – there was nothing green, no houses, no tents, no shade. At one point fresh tar was put onto the road and my scooter slid. Before I knew what was happening, I was lying in the black sticky mess. The workmen thought the spectacle terribly funny (Sigrid also killed herself laughing). The men then brought rags and gas and tried to get the tar off my clothes. It took a long time before I was even halfway presentable again.

We were happy to reach Cairo, a big, busy, modern city. The Nile is quite wide there and on its banks were modern high-rises. We went to the youth hostel, which was a lovely house surrounded by a nice garden. We were the only guests, except for some bedbugs we tried to ignore. We stayed there three days.

Our first sightseeing tour led us to the pyramids. That was a busy place full of camels, Arabs and tourists – all were noisy. The pyramids looked very impressive. To think that they had stood there for several thousand years was awe-inspiring. The Sphinx was partly covered by scaffolding when we visited, but we could recognize her quite well. The whole pyramid complex was at the edge of the desert, a hot and dusty place.

We left Cairo to travel to the southern part of Egypt. The trip was enjoyable in the rich Nile River Valley. We just followed the river. In some spots the Nile was as wide as three kilometres, in others much narrower. The change from rich farmland to desert was radical. One could literally stand with one foot in a garden and the other in the desert.

When we reached Beni Suef, Sigrid's scooter didn't want to go any further. Consequently, we decided to leave the scooters behind and travel by bus. Since we had to go to the police station anyway in order to register, we asked if we could leave the scooters for a few days. This simple question caused quite a bit of excitement. But after we had sat down and drank some hot, back, sweet coffee with the policemen, they said they would be delighted to look after our scooters. When we parted they insisted on sending with us two men to carry our packs and to show us the way to the bus station.

The bus took us to the city of Minya, where the police were waiting for us again. We showed them our passports and marched out of town to find a place to camp. We hadn't gone very far when the police followed in a car and insisted we go with them to the police station. This we did. But the police chief wasn't there, so they took us to another place where no one could read our passports either. We were a little angry by then. To placate us, coffee was ordered and then we were taken to the edge of town. When the police heard we were planning to camp, they almost had a fit. But, seeing that we were serious, they took us to a garden surrounded by a wall and appointed a guard to watch over us. We put up our tent, made supper and tea and invited our guard to partake, which he was delighted to do. I woke up in the middle of the night and thought a camel or donkey was nibbling at our tent. Turned out it was the guard sitting on a mat, chewing sugar cane.

The next morning, as we were walking along the road, a Greek Orthodox bishop stopped and offered us a ride in his beautiful car. He was an interesting person and told us a lot about Egypt and its political and economic problems. He also told us that a recent war with Great Britain and the consequent hate propaganda had made travelling for white people somewhat dangerous. The owner of a grocery store took us another few miles along, between fields of sugar cane. Then we walked again, followed by dozens of children and even some grown-ups. An old man offered us his donkey to ride on, which we thought was very kind. People there had a hard time figuring out why "rich Europeans" would walk and carry heavy packs.

Soon a chauffeur-driven car stopped and a very fat man offered us a ride. He was a well-to-do landowner and insisted on taking us to his house. This was a pleasant place, with large trees and a swimming pool. We very much enjoyed a good swim. Later lunch was served, and then the chauffeur took us to Asyut to a relative of our fat man. We were quite surprised when we arrived at an estate and were welcomed by three unmarried brothers and sisters who seemed to live there. We admired the huge garden, the fountain, the palace-like house, the large rooms full of beautiful furniture, Persian carpets and pictures. We were given a room with a high ceiling, an enormous chandelier and two beds with canopies over them. The highlight was an all-marble modern bathroom with fixtures that even worked. We were impressed.

As soon as we were cleaned up, we were shown the town, and then had tea at one place and dinner at another. As always everyone asked us the same questions. But it was worth it. Sleeping in clean, soft beds in a cool room felt wonderful. In the morning there was a soft knock at the door and a servant brought breakfast on a silver tray. Later we chatted in the garden with the owners of the place. Then we were shown the Coptic monastery at the edge of town. Lunch was again at somebody's house, which was followed by a yacht trip on the Nile. By the time we got back we were a bit tired of our hosts and their friends. They were a strange type of people – they all seemed to have something wrong with them. One was cross-eyed, the next didn't look at people when he talked to them and the third laughed like a crazy person. And none of them knew what to do to combat their boredom.

We decided to take the evening train to Luxor. Our hosts wanted us to stay longer, but we felt it was time to go. A train trip in Egypt is definitely something special. The windows in our compartment were cross-barred and the door locked from the outside. Every once in a while someone unlocked the door and wanted to see our tickets, or did some dusting, or wanted to sell tea. And everyone asked for a baksheesh. We finally stretched out in our sleeping bags and slept. In the morning several railway officials told us we had arrived in Luxor. They all wanted money for providing this "service."

We crossed the Nile and settled down in the dirty, flea-ridden pension of Sheikh Ali. There were fleas and bedbugs everywhere, but the worst were the flies. The eyes and noses of young children and old people were often completely covered with flies. It was quite depressing. And then a person couldn't make a move without being asked for baksheesh. "Baksheesh" seemed to be every second word, and we were helpless victims.

We were now in the desert. It was terribly hot there and dusty. It never rained. We were almost afraid of getting sunstroke, since we had no hats. When we met an Arab alone in the desert, we felt uncomfortable. Justified or not, we'd heard so many horror stories about Arab men. We decided not to go out at night, and even during the day to stay as close together as possible.

However, the city of Luxor was wonderful in spite of all the shortcomings. We walked about the sites of ancient Thebes and admired the great temple and its most striking feature, the Great Colonnade. We also stood in awe in front of the colossal statues and again wished we were more knowledgeable about ancient history and culture.

We went to see the terrace temple of Queen Hatshepsut, the walls of which are adorned with scenes from her expedition to Puone (Somaliland) in search of incense trees. One morning we went to the Valley of the Queens, where the royal relatives of the 20th dynasty were buried. Another day we went to the Valley of the Kings, where, in 1922, the completely intact tomb of Tutankhamen was found. We were immensely impressed with the wall paintings in some of the tombs only recently discovered. The colours were still so fresh and so vibrant. It made us think the walls had been painted only a short while ago, not thousands of years ago. The pictures were amazingly vital and full of energy and gave an idea of what life was like during that time. Even the writing looked like a picture book. Often figures were carved into the rock or brought out in relief form. It was very quiet in the Valley of the Kings. The buzzing of the flies was about the only sound there. Then there were the white stones and the white sand and bright hot sun.

After a few days in Luxor, we were so tired that we took the train back to Asyut and travelled to Beni Suef, where we picked up our scooters. It had been an interesting trip but a different one, mainly because of the heat, the general poverty and the people. The poor people were poorer than any we had ever met, and the rich seemed quite corrupt and self-satisfied. We didn't meet anyone in between. We both wanted to be among other people again, people like the friendly Mexicans or Japanese or our friends on the German freighter.

Back in Cairo we spent a couple of days at the museum, which was full of lovely and amazing sculptures. We saw lots of different mosques and the City of the Dead, which is a huge place where hundreds of generations of Egyptians are buried. We met a young man who wanted to marry one of us but couldn't decide which one. We each in turn praised our own beauty, intelligence and whatever else we could think of. When he still couldn't make up his mind, I asked if he could not just marry both of us since he was a Muslim. "Would you really become my wives?" was his delighted reply.

From Cairo, we followed the desert road to Alexandria, where we stayed for a week. Alexandria, founded by Alexander the Great around 300 BC, was quite a modern city right by the Mediterranean Sea. Part of the city was built on a peninsula and surrounded on three sides by ocean. One day there was a storm and as we drove along the water we were almost blown off our scooters. The climate was so much better there than inland, and we enjoyed the steady breeze from the Mediterranean. As always we met a lot of people and were taken from one party to another. We were invited to come to the sports club as guests and enjoyed swimming in the pool. We also went sailing and played golf. We really enjoyed the sailing as the waves were quite high and a strong wind was blowing.

From Alexandria we wanted to travel to Israel, but since Egypt and Israel were enemies there were no ships going to Israel. Neither did we get a permit for the land route. We finally ended up travelling as deck passengers on an Egyptian ship to Syria. When it got dark, Sigrid and I put up our tent among the freight on deck. It wasn't easy to find enough room, but we managed and had a peaceful night. In the morning everyone was astonished to see us crawl out of the tent, and crew as well as passengers came to see our "house." During the second night we had quite a storm and many passengers got sick. The smell below deck was horrific. We were so glad we had our own place in the fresh air on deck.

It rained when we arrived in Syria, the first rain we'd had in six months. We could have done without. We liked Syria. The people were so different from the Egyptians; they seemed prouder and happier. I wondered if this had anything to do with the climate. It was cooler in Syria and there were mountains, such a lovely change from the desert. Spring had also arrived. The Syrian men wore strange black pants, a lot like riding pants, wide on top and quite narrow from the knee down.

From Syria we drove into Turkey, a place we liked from the beginning. There were high mountains, most of them still covered with snow. In the valleys trees were blossoming, grass was green, and yellow and blue irises, crocuses and daisies were blooming. It was almost like home. On the first evening in Turkey my tire blew and we went to the next village to have it fixed. The garage was already closed, so some farmers immediately took our scooters and put them in a safe place. We were invited into a farmhouse, where a big pot of steaming bread soup stood on the floor. Bread, cheese and olives lay next to it. Everyone got a spoon and settled around the soup pot and started eating. It was wonderful to get something hot into the stomach. Later we sat around a fire on the floor in the living room and tried to make conversation. That wasn't easy. Luckily, one of the men spoke a little French.

We just loved the harbour town of Iskenderun. Everything seemed so clean and friendly there. We also liked Adana, a pretty town surrounded by mountains. Less likeable was the weather. We had become so used to warm or hot cloudless days that we found it hard to put up with the rain and cold. North of Adana, we really got to where the spring flowers bloomed. On the second day we reached the high plateau of Turkey that stretches for hundreds of kilometres. But it was cold! We put on everything we possessed, which wasn't enough. For gloves we used our spare socks. When it wasn't raining we even draped our sleeping bags over our shoulders in an effort to stay warm. I'm sure we looked very strange. For the first time we met some German fellows. They were travelling south and we were almost envious because we had to go further and further north.

Just before we reached Istanbul, my machine stopped. After taking it apart I realized that one of the piston rings had broken and damaged the piston. What now? A kind truck driver loaded our scooters and us into his truck and drove us to Istanbul. We tried for days to get spare parts, without success. Finally, we went to Pan American Airways, the only airline that flew to Tokyo. We asked if they would take a letter to Tokyo for us. In the letter we asked our motor scooter firm for a new piston, which the airline promised to fly back as soon as possible.

APRIL 1958

We liked Istanbul, a city built on many hills along the Bosporus. From one of the mountains on the Asiatic side we could see the Sea of Marmara, which stretched all the way to the horizon. We could also see the narrow strip of water, the Bosporus, which connects the Sea of Marmara with the Black Sea. Delightful to the eye were the many mosques and minarets all over the city. How beautiful it would have been to be there in the summer.

Since we had to wait for our scooter parts, we decided to try a little hitchhiking round trip. It was a beautiful day as we drove along the Sea of Marmara to a small town called Izmit, where fruit trees and spring flowers were in full bloom. The next day we went on to Bursa, where we had been told there was a ski area. Well there was no snow anywhere near, and we were told we had to go to a place called

Uludag, high up in the mountains, to find that "white stuff." Everyone we talked to tried to talk us out of going, and we were told stories of wolves and bad people.

Of course, this only encouraged us all the more, so we started walking. A truck picked us up and took us a few kilometres, and then we walked again. After a while we got out of the fog into the most beautiful sunshine. We were delighted when we saw the first snow, which increased as we gained altitude. After a while a tractor picked us up and took us along until it got stuck in the snow. We had to walk again through deep snow until we finally reached Uludag, a Turkish ski area. It was beautiful there, and even though it was already late afternoon we rented some skis and boots and hiked up the next hill. Gliding down was utter joy.

In the hotel where we had rented the skis, we met a lot of people. A man offered us his hut to stay in. He said he only used it in the summer. That suited us well. We now had our own home! We made a fire, cooked some soup, cleaned the place up a bit and went to sleep. We were tired. It was very cold when we woke up. I offered to get out of the warm sleeping bag to make a fire. After a good breakfast we started to climb the highest mountain in the area, Uludag. It was still early, 6 a.m., and the snow was still frozen. And we could carry our skis almost all the way to the top, which we reached at noon.

We had a wonderful view over the hills and snow-covered mountain peaks around us. We even saw the Sea of Marmara from the top and several lakes. There was a cold wind blowing and we began our descent. The first section was quite steep and icy, but then the fun began and we simply had a marvellous time skiing down the mountain.

We were quite tired when we reached our cabin. We just weren't in shape anymore; riding scooters all the time had turned us into softies. We collected water, made a fire, cooked, ate and cleaned up. Suddenly, there was a knock at the door. In came a good-looking Turkish man. He gave us a friendly smile, said hello and, talking constantly, went into the kitchen to make tea. We didn't know what was going on. A little while later the owner of the cabin came and with him a whole bunch of people. We had a party, which was later continued at the hotel. We heard then that the next day was Easter and wondered if the Easter bunny would show up in Turkey.

The party at the hotel was fun. When we went home we were a bit astonished that Mustafa, our mysterious Turk, came home with us and moved into one of the spare bedrooms. Early in the morning we heard Mustafa rummaging around in the kitchen. When we got up the fire was lit, the table set and Mustafa served us delicious coffee. Bread, butter and honey were already on the table. After breakfast Mustafa tried to teach us Turkish and we were willing pupils.

We went skiing again and joined some Austrians we had met at the party the night before. One of them injured his ankle and I skied down to get a toboggan for him. By the time we had him back at the hotel we had the ski area to ourselves. When we returned to our hut, Mustafa had already set the table and started cooking a fantastic meal. After dinner we had to learn Turkish again before going with Mustafa to another hut, where we played games and drank *raki*, Turkish schnapps.

It was raining the following day when we left this wonderful place after lunch, much to the regret of our dear Mustafa. We hitchhiked back to Bursa and from there to Izmir. There was little traffic and our progress was slow. But we didn't mind; the country was beautiful and the people very friendly and hospitable. Often regular buses stopped for us but refused to take our money. Our co-travellers asked us many questions and always insisted we share their meals with them.

We loved Izmir (known as Smyrna in ancient times). The harbour was attractive, and we were astonished to see two German freighters anchored there. We took a room in a small hotel, but there were so many bugs that we removed all the bedding and slept in our sleeping bags. We stayed two days in Izmir then took a bus to the Cesme Peninsula, which had a magnificent fortress. We camped right on top of the fortress hill, met some young Germans, made a big fire and sang half the night away.

We had just fallen asleep when an enormous thunderstorm woke us up. I was barely asleep again when Sigrid yelled, "Get away!" Some men tried to get into our tent and we had a hard time discouraging them. Luckily, they finally left. Early in the morning we heard some more movement around the tent, but we didn't bother to look and soon it was quiet again. When we finally got up there were fresh buns and fruit left in front of the tent. We made coffee and had a good breakfast.

We packed up and walked down to the harbour where a small Greek ship had anchored. We asked the captain if he would take us to the next island, Chios. The captain said yes, but he charged an outrageous price. We bargained for about three hours and even walked off once or twice. We eventually agreed on a mutually acceptable sum. The relatively short trip in the small boat was fun. The waves were quite high and more than once washed over us.

From Chios we took a larger ship across the Aegean Sea to Piraeus, Greece. We slept on deck and arrived the next morning. We found a tiny youth hostel and a truly funny hostel father. He kept telling us jokes and thought everything we said was funny. We came just in time for Easter, which in Greece is a week later than in Turkey. This time we got our share of Easter eggs.

After we had looked at Athens and climbed up to the Acropolis, we decided to make a short round trip through Greece. We just loved the people and the country. Everyone was so friendly and the country-side so beautiful. If we asked a farmer if we could camp on his property, he usually insisted that we sleep in his best room, and he and his family would also share their meals with us. Easter is the biggest holiday of the year in Greece. The day after Good Friday there was a big procession and at midnight everyone, even the queen of Greece, went to mass to celebrate the Resurrection. Then the feasting began, which started with a soup made from the innards of the Easter lamb and Easter bread baked with a red egg inside. On Easter Sunday people ate the Easter lamb. Everywhere we went we had to try bread, lamb, eggs and wine. Often we were stopped as we walked along the road, and we had to sit down with the men (many of whom had been to America and worked there for a number of years and spoke good English) to drink wine and talk.

One day a farmer's wife insisted we come with her to visit a sick priest. We went but felt somewhat idiotic sitting by the bedside of an old man without being able to talk to him. The orthodox priests in this land didn't cut their hair, and all had long beards and long hair, mostly worn in one braid hanging down their back. They were allowed to marry before they became priests but not after. Only those who were single could advance in the church.

We looked at many antique places and again regretted our ignorance of past history. We saw Corinth, the mountain city, with its antique columns and beautiful museum. We were fascinated with the well-preserved theatre in Epidaurus and impressed by the old city of Mycenae, with its fortress and tombs and the superb Lion Gate. We hitchhiked to Sparta and Mystras, which we thought absolutely beautiful. Mystras is a city of the dead and built into a mountain. We also looked at the ruins of houses, a palace and a fortress. There were at least six ancient churches, some of them still well preserved, full of frescoes and old pictures. In between all the beautiful architecture were wildflowers, bushes and trees so lush and green we wanted to stay there forever.

In Olympia we admired Hermes, the most beautiful man in the world, according to some Australian girls. We also admired the location where the first Olympic Games took place and some fallen ruins. We were delighted with the small town of Nafplion, with its huge fortress on top of a mountain and another on a little island in the sea. The latter had been turned into a prison and afterwards a luxury hotel.

Greece is an amazing country. Everything there was green and blooming. The orange and lemon trees were laden with fruit, and the smells of flowers and trees were intoxicating. After the heat and sparse vegetation in India and Egypt, Greece seemed like paradise to us. There were few cars there and we often spent hours lying in the grass waiting for a ride. But we didn't mind as we had lots of time. We enjoyed not having to tell everyone our life's story. When we told people we were from Germany, they assumed we came directly from there to Greece and not around the globe via North America, India and Turkey.

On the last day on the Peloponnese, we almost drowned. It rained all day and we camped under a bridge. During the night the water in the creek rose by several metres and we had to flee. It was quite scary and not a bit funny. Luckily, we found an empty house where we dried off and spent the rest of the night.

Back in Athens we got a visa for Yugoslavia and were just on our way to leave the city when we were almost run over by the king, who came around a corner way above the speed limit. Well, His Majesty had to put on the brakes for us. From the capital we hitchhiked to Delphi, where we spent the evening in a small village taking part in a fiesta and drinking retsina wine and eating bread and lamb.

When we finally moved on it was completely dark and had started to rain. After walking quite a distance we saw a house that seemed empty. We quietly opened the door and asked if anybody was home. Nobody answered. We lit a match and found a small table and, to our delight, a candle. Only after the candle was lit did we realize we were in a church. Hoping a priest or his parishioners wouldn't wake us up, we slept peacefully. On we went to Delphi, which we loved. The Greeks really knew how to pick the best places for their cities. It was early in the morning and everything was fresh and green and sunny.

Just before we reached Thessaloniki, the second-biggest city in Greece, we crossed a beautiful mountain range. We had planned to hike up the almost 3000-metre-high Mount Olympus, but we didn't feel like stopping anymore. We were beginning to look forward to getting back home to Germany. We found Kavala a beautiful city situated between the ocean and the mountains. One part of the city is an island and connected with the other part by a huge aqueduct. Two musicians gave us a lift, one Greek, the other Spanish. They picked up a lady pianist in Alexandroupolis, where the three of them were giving a concert. We got free tickets and enjoyed a perfect Sunday with great music and lovely people. After the concert a special dinner was served for the musicians and we were also invited to join in. The food was tremendous. Ricardo, the Spaniard, kept telling jokes, like the one about the skinny lady who ate an olive and swallowed the pit by mistake, whereupon everyone thought she was pregnant!

MAY 1958

We got back to Istanbul and found a lovely and inexpensive hotel outside the city with a gorgeous view of the ocean. From our window we watched dolphins frolicking in the water. I spent most of the day at the customs office, trying to get the parts for my scooter that had arrived. The customs officer wanted me to pay 66 liras in duties, but I managed to get it down to 25. It didn't take us long to build in the new parts and once again my scooter performed well. While we were at it, we also did some maintenance work on Sigrid's scooter.

Istanbul is such a wonderful city, even though it was quite cold. There was so much to see: the Blue Mosque, the impressive Hagia Sophia church with its huge dome and mosaics, the museums, the bazaars. We also went to see the palace of Sultan Ahmed and the Great Palace Mosaic Museum and spent a lot of time just driving around the city.

And then, one Sunday afternoon, we left Istanbul. Somehow we felt sad, as if our journey around the world had come to an end. But there was really nothing to be sad about. The sun was shining and every day was becoming warmer. First we packed the mitts (socks) away, then the scarves, and after a while we didn't even need jackets anymore.

We entered Bulgaria and found the people there not only extremely friendly but also very interested in our journey. Everyone wanted to know where we came from and what we had seen. Only the police were a bit too nosy. At the border we had to unpack our packsacks (which were a bit grubby by now) and everything we owned (also grubby) was given close scrutiny. On the road we were stopped in every village for passport control. One day we were eating our bread and drinking our water a few kilometres outside a village when we saw a policeman bicycling toward us. I quickly prepared a slice of bread and handed it to him when he arrived. Sigrid gave him a cup of water and told him to sit down with us. The poor man was so embarrassed that he didn't ask for our passports. He smiled, thanked us and rode back to where he came from. We were amazed at how empty the roads were in Bulgaria. There were barely any cars. The stores were also almost empty. We wondered how people managed with so little.

Sofia was a pleasant town. We didn't want to stay long, but we met Ivan from the Automobile Club and a high-ranking communist lady who called us comrades. Both talked us into staying a few days. We were taken to a nice hotel, at government expense, and had our visa extended. The evening we spent with Ivan and his friend Entscho. First we had dinner, then we danced and drank lots of good Bulgarian wine. We enjoyed ourselves. The only thing that bothered us was the fact that the police watched us at all times.

The next day Ivan and Entscho showed us the city. They were riding on the backs of our scooters and the police were amused. The press interviewed us and we had our pictures taken, which pleased our lady comrade. Everyone was so nice to us that we hated to leave. For a farewell gift our lady comrade gave us two big Bulgarian sausages and a carved wooden plate each. We had to promise to come back soon. It didn't take us long to reach the border and then we were in Yugoslavia.

The dust on the unpaved roads in Yugoslavia reminded us of Japan. Only after we reached Belgrade did we have a paved road all the way to Zagreb. We spent the night at a university hostel then moved on to the Rijeka port on the Adriatic Sea. We loved being near an ocean again and also met a lot of people who wanted us to stay. But we were restless; we were so close to home now and wanted to get there as soon as possible. We drove back to Zagreb and a day later we were in Graz, Austria. We were so excited to be in a German-speaking country that we talked with everyone who asked us questions. We also bought some delicious sausages and apples and even pastries in one of those incredible Austrian pastry shops. It was fun spending some of our last dollars.

We liked Vienna so much that we stayed there an extra day. Not only the city but also the surroundings were indeed beautiful. In Linz we stopped to visit Hans Gmoser, our friend from Banff, who was supposed to be home from Canada for a holiday. But he hadn't arrived yet. Still, we spent a pleasant evening with his relatives.

The following day we entered Germany. After an absence of three years we were home again. We camped for the last time in a farmer's field near Nuremberg. We had mixed feelings on this last evening together. On one hand we were looking forward to coming home, on the other this was the end of an incredibly good chapter in our lives.

After breakfast we ceremoniously built a fire and burned or buried everything we owned – except what we wore. Near Würzburg, it started to rain and got quite chilly. In Hanau the sun came out again and we kept going until we reached Frankfurt. At the Hauptbahnhof (main railroad station) we separated and drove to our families' homes, where we were eagerly awaited.

It was good to be home again.

At least for a little while.

A LIFE OF TRAVEL

It didn't take us long to get used to being home again. I got a job as a kindergarten teacher and enjoyed being with the little ones. Sigrid took a course to become a midwife. We often met to talk about our new lives.

Early in 1959 I got a call from our friend Hans Gmoser, who was visiting in Austria. He asked me if I would cook for him again at Little Yoho and travel there with him the following month. I liked the idea, so I quit my job, and Hans and I took a plane to Montreal and from there to Calgary. Our friend Leo picked us up and drove us to Banff and later to Field, where we hiked up to Little Yoho. While Hans and Leo were busy bringing up supplies, I had my hands full with cleaning up the place, arranging bedding and cooking. Soon the first guests arrived and we enjoyed the powder skiing throughout the area. One day we made a long tour and ended up toward evening in a hut nearby, named Twin Falls. I liked the place immediately and when the skiing was over I asked if I could rent it. It belonged to a guy named Brewster, and he let me have it for 40 dollars for the rest of the year. I was delighted.

I advertised Twin Falls as a guest house and spent some time cleaning it up, buying sheets and making beds. Some pack rats had spent the winter in the cabin, and it took me quite a while to get rid of them with the help of Hans. I also spent time carrying up supplies, which wasn't easy. I bought what I needed in Field, BC. To get back from there, I had to hitchhike ten kilometres to Takakkaw Falls and then hike for about two hours back to Twin Falls with a heavy pack on my back. I cooked, baked, looked after my guests and did a lot of hiking in the area. The summer passed by too quickly, and then it was time to go back to Germany again. It was nice to see my family and Sigrid once more.

I had liked Twin Falls so much that in the spring of 1960 I returned. A young man by the name of Felix came up and we did quite a bit of hiking together. One day he asked if I'd like to climb Mount Assiniboine with him – something I'd longed to do since 1957. I said I would, left the cabin with a friend and off we went. It was a long but beautiful hike into the Assiniboine Valley, where we spent the night with Lizzy Rummel in her cabin. The next day we did the climb, which was arduous but lovely, and the view from the top was heavenly. Then Felix asked me if I would marry him and I said yes. I liked the guy. We got married on September 26, in Field, BC, and had a big party afterwards in Banff. Sigrid got married in Freiburg on the same day to a fellow called Gerhard. My parents attended her wedding.

Felix had bought a new Volkswagen Bug, and for our honeymoon we decided to drive to South America to do some climbing in the

Andes. Felix had arranged the seats so we could sleep in the car quite comfortably. We left Banff in November, travelled through deep snow in Yellowstone Park, hiked into the Grand Canyon and drove on to Mexico. We visited with all my friends there and spent some time hiking up the Popocatépetl and Iztaccíhuatl. Felix had never done this and loved it.

We then drove through Central America on dirt roads, spending Christmas in Nicaragua. We camped near a lake and Felix did some work on the Volkswagen. Then we took two little kids, who had been watching us, to town to buy them some Christmas presents. The next thing we knew, their mother arrived with a live chicken as our Christmas present. Since I had no clue how to prepare it, I had to return it.

It was very hot when we finally arrived in Panama, the end of the road. We left the car there and flew to Lima, Peru, and from there took a bus to Cusco, a lovely old town. I realized by then I was pregnant, so we gave up on our climbing plans but still went on to Machu Picchu, the holy city high in the Andes. Except for some llamas, we were the only visitors and enjoyed the place to the fullest. Eventually, we went back to Lima, then flew to Panama, got our car and drove back to Canada after an absence of six months.

The next few years kept us busy settling down and having babies. We made several trips to Germany to show off my family to my parents and to Sigrid and Gerhard, who had also increased their family. In 1963 we moved to Castlegar, BC, where Felix got a job as an electrician and where we built a house. Once the children started school I got a job teaching kindergarten. Together as a family we made many hiking and skiing trips. Felix loved his mountains and wanted the children to enjoy them as much as he did. And they did.

In 1985 I read an advertisement about a trip to the Hunza Valley in Pakistan. Ever since I had read about Hunza as a teenager I'd wanted to go there. I'd read that the Hunza people enjoyed incredible longevity because of their diet, climate and lack of social stress, not to mention the exercise of climbing up and down the steep mountainsides to tend their plots of land. The Hunzas are said to be descendants of five wandering soldiers from Alexander the Great's army.

I booked the trip, flew to Frankfurt and from there to Islamabad. I met my six travel companions there and we drove 1200 kilometres on the Karakoram Highway to Gilgit, the gateway to Hunza. The Karakoram Highway, then only seven years old, took 20 years to be built. At the peak of construction it employed 15,000 Pakistanis and 10,000 Chinese workers. It claims the world's most unstable terrain, due to glacial shifts, brittle rock, earthquakes and extremes in temperature (up to 50 degrees Celsius in the summer and -30 in the winter). Most of the way, the paved highway clings to the steep gorge of the Indus River, a rushing stream of muddy water sometimes as much as 700 metres below the road. The further north we went there were fewer signs of human life or vegetation. But we had some magnificent views of snow-capped mountains, among them the 8126-metre Nanga Parbat.

From Gilgit we followed the Hunza River for 100 kilometres north to Ali Abad. The highway was carved into the walls of the Hunza Gorge – the only gorge that actually cuts through the Karakoram mountain range. This drive was the most beautiful and spectacular I had ever taken. We went up steep mountain switchbacks and crossed narrow wooden bridges over deep canyons. Immense snow-capped mountains towered over us. The village of Ali Abad, with fruit-laden apricot trees, was a typical green oasis in an otherwise grey landscape. In golden wheat fields, women were cutting the stalks with sickles. The most awful road, little but a rocky trail, forced us to walk on the steepest pitches. But it delivered us to Karimabad, the capital of the state of Hunza (altitude 2500 metres). Every flat surface featured apricots, laid out in single layers to dry in the sun. Apricots form the main diet of the Hunza people.

We hiked up to Baltit Fort, which used to be the home of the Mir (ruler) of Hunza until 1945. The core of the fort dates back to the eighth century AD. It was now a crumbling structure of stones, dried mud and timber. However, it had beautifully carved wooden doors, window frames and beams to hold up the place. From the fort we had magical views of Mount Ultar, over 7000 metres high, covered with huge glaciers, and across the valley to Mount Rakaposhi, even higher, which seemed to grow right into the sky.

The houses of Karimabad and other villages squeezed tightly up against the mountain slopes and each other to conserve what little room there was for agriculture. Hunza was experiencing problems with overcrowding due to road accessibility and better ways of conquering disease. It's not the completely isolated place it once was.

After spending a week in Hunza, meeting people and eating apricots, we left this enchanting spot for a ten-day trek into the Batura Mountains. Then it was time to fly home.

The following year I was invited to travel with some Swiss people to Ladakh and Zanskar in Kashmir. We flew to the city of Srinagar and from there travelled by car over huge mountain passes to Ladakh. We saw beautiful scenery, outstanding monasteries like Lamayuru, and lovely palaces in and around the capital of Leh.

The best part, however, was our trek to Zanskar. Our car left us at a snow-covered, 4500-metre pass and my six Swiss lady friends, our Swiss guide and I started hiking. Our porters carried our camping gear on horses and also carried live chickens and other things to feed us with. The country was incredibly wild, treeless and beautiful. Fast rivers flowed everywhere, and few even had homemade bridges. There were some villages, and the people there urged us to stop and talk to them. One night we camped at 5000 metres and the next morning got up at 4 a.m. to climb a nearby "hill" just so we could say we'd been as high as 6000 metres.

The highlight of the trip was a visit to the Phuktal Monastery, which was built into a cliff at 4000 metres elevation. To get there we had to hike along a river with blue poppies everywhere. A fresh breeze was blowing and life was good. We had to cross another raging river on a bridge with no handrails but made it safely.

The first view of Phuktal was breathtaking – a whole cluster of little white buildings stuck to the surface of a cliff with a huge cave on top. Two dozen chortens (shrines), stairs and tunnels led us to the buildings that housed the Buddhist monks. We were given a friendly reception and shown the place from top to bottom. The cave above the monastery extended 20 metres above our heads like a perfectly proportioned cupola. The view from the unprotected edge of the cave cliff was magnificent, with the river, a village, fields and mountains as far as the eye could see. Before we left the monks served us tea. We were all reluctant to leave. I felt if I hadn't seen anything but Phuktal, the trip would have still been worthwhile.

Later on in the trip we met two tourists – the only ones. One of them looked at me and said, "Hi Renate." He was the guide from the previous year's trip. You never know who you'll meet, even in the wilderness! We had to cross another high pass before finally descending. We also had to cross a fast, waist-deep river. Our brave guide went first, tied to a rope, and one by one we all followed to the other side, completely drenched.

We eventually made it back to India. We spent some time in Delhi then flew home. I hated to say goodbye to all my Swiss friends, but it was also nice to be home again.

The following year, in 1987, I got together with two of my Swiss friends from the previous year and we set out to explore Tibet and China. We met in Frankfurt, flew to Kathmandu in Nepal and continued from there by bus. I found Kathmandu very changed from when I was there 30 years ago; there were new roads, new buildings and thousands of cars. However, it was still a lovely spot to see and enjoy.

It took two days to travel by slow bus on dirt roads to the border of Tibet. From there we went over high passes, one 5200 metres, on even slower buses to Shigatse and Gyangze, two of the few beautiful monasteries not destroyed by the Chinese. From there it was on to the Brahmaputra Valley. A brand new bridge brought us across the river and shortly afterwards we reached Lhasa. I still couldn't quite believe it! How many have dreamed of Lhasa and how few have reached it. How could I have been so lucky and privileged?

My first impressions of Lhasa weren't so favourable. We saw nothing but ugly Chinese cement-block buildings. But the centre of town was more Tibetan and friendlier looking. Once we saw the Potala Palace dominating the old town, our excitement knew no bounds. The Potala was built of wood, stone and earth, has 13 storeys and was completed in 1694. It has over 1,000 rooms, 10,000 shrines and 20,000 statues.

We entered the Potala by a series of wide stone steps and followed other pilgrims from room to room, chapel to chapel. We were amazed at all the statues, the darkness of the rooms, the thousands of evil-smelling butter lamps and the devotion of the Tibetans. From the roof of the Potala we had a wonderful view of Lhasa and the surrounding mountains. The old town, with the golden roofs of the Jokhang Temple Monastery in the middle, was visibly different from the new town built by the Chinese in the '50s.

We spent almost a week in Lhasa trying to see as much as possible. One day we rented bikes and rode to the Drepung Monastery, another place worth seeing. But then it was time to go. We left by bus for Golmud, 1100 kilometres northeast, and rode again over a high plateau with some passes reaching over 5000 metres. The trip took two days. After a day of rest, we went to see Dunhuang, the start of the Silk Road. The city is famous for its caves full of Buddhist scriptures, ancient manuscripts, silk scroll paintings and statues, each one more beautiful than the next.

In the evening we travelled by camel over huge sand dunes to Yueya (Crescent Moon) Lake, a beautiful spot in the desert. Then we continued travelling over 2000 kilometres all the way to Kashgar. It was a difficult trip, as the Chinese at the time only catered to foreigners travelling in groups. Most hotels refused to let us stay, and even food in restaurants was often denied the three of us. One night, after having tried many hotels, we took out our sleeping bags and settled down to sleep in the lobby of the last hotel we'd tried. Very quickly the manager arrived and said he'd found us a room.

We loved Kashgar, the westernmost city in China, and spent a week among friendly people, seeing all the sights worth seeing and having a great time. We then bought tickets to fly back to Beijing, with a stop in Xi'an to see the terracotta warriors. After a few days in Beijing my friends flew back to Switzerland and I landed back home in Canada.

In 1988 I travelled by myself to spend part of the summer in Guatemala and Belize. The next year I travelled with Helen and Hedi, my two Swiss friends from the China trip, to Ecuador and the Galapagos. In Ecuador we did a lot of mountain climbing but also enjoyed a canoe trip on one of the rivers in the jungle. In the capital city of Quito, I phoned Sepp Dubach, the cheese maker I'd met in the Langtang Valley in Nepal over 30 years before. In 1962 Sepp had visited Felix and me in Canada. We had a wonderful reunion in Ecuador. Sepp and his family had a lovely home, and he was still making cheese.*

We then flew 1600 kilometres across the Pacific to the Galapagos Islands. A guide met us at the airport and took us to a waiting ship. We travelled every day to a different island and saw the most wonderful wildlife and scenery. The Galapagos are truly a place worth visiting.

Looking back these past years at all the travel I have enjoyed to the fullest, I am still amazed at how many countries Sigrid and I journeyed through, how many things of beauty we saw and how many wonderful

* Tragically, in 1994 thieves who had broken into his house murdered both Sepp and his son.

people we met. Those trips sparked my desire to keep on travelling and see new places. Luckily, I worked as a teacher and had the summers off to do just that.

Of all the places I've visited, the Himalayas were my favourite. I loved the mountains, the villages and the high passes we crossed, and I have continued trekking there. I have also travelled to Europe, visiting relatives, skiing in the Alps, taking a boat trip on the Volga, exploring parts of Russia and visiting Scandinavia. I have also returned to China and India and visited quite a few places in Africa.

Seeing new places, and meeting new people, gives me a lot of pleasure and satisfaction. I intend to keep exploring our beautiful world – it is always well worth it.